Fathead Goes to Chico

Mitch Cox

iUniverse, Inc.
New York Lincoln Shanghai

Fathead Goes to Chico

iUniverse books may be ordered through booksellers or by contacting:

iUniverse
2021 Pine Lake Road, Suite 100
Lincoln, NE 68512
www.iuniverse.com
1-800-Authors (1-800-288-4677)

ISBN: 978-0-595-46565-1 (pbk)
ISBN: 978-0-595-90861-5 (ebk)

Printed in the United States of America

Fathead Goes to Chico

For Laura, with love, for all
the years of patience and understanding.

"That's what college is for—getting as many bad decisions as possible out of the way before you're forced into the real world."

—J. Jacques

Contents

Prologue 1

CHAPTER 1 3

CHAPTER 2 7

CHAPTER 3 11

CHAPTER 4 13

CHAPTER 5 19

CHAPTER 6 24

CHAPTER 7 32

CHAPTER 8 39

CHAPTER 9 43

CHAPTER 10 48

CHAPTER 11 51

CHAPTER 12 54

CHAPTER 13 65

CHAPTER 14 73

CHAPTER 15 75

CHAPTER 16 79

CHAPTER 17 84

CHAPTER 18 88

CHAPTER 19.. 95

CHAPTER 20 98

CHAPTER 21.. 102

CHAPTER 22 108

CHAPTER 23.. 113

CHAPTER 24 118

CHAPTER 25.. 127

CHAPTER 26 132

CHAPTER 27 137

CHAPTER 28 141

Fathead (fat-hed) *n* 1. *slang;* a stupid or naïve person; fool synonyms: goof, goofball, bozo, jackass, cuckoo, sap

Prologue

I started writing this book just a few years after I graduated from Chico State. I was going through a rough time in my life, and this was a way for me to remember happier times. As I wrote, I realized these were not only happier times, but in looking back, these were the most memorable times of my life.

I have worked at colleges for nearly twenty years now, and whenever I have the opportunity to speak to a group of students, I make a point of saying this to them:

Look around you. Look at the people sitting next to you. Look at the people that you live with. These are your friends, and they will always be your friends. Even if years from now, when you have no idea where they are, or what they're doing—they will always be your friends; because you will always remember them, and they will always remember you. You will never experience another time like this in your life. Cherish it. Treasure it. Enjoy it. Remember it.

There are occasions in the book, where I may exaggerate, or embellish. This is done, hopefully, in the name of humour. I have also slightly changed the names of the people that I met along the way out of respect for their privacy. But they know who they are. And I hope they know what they meant to me.

1

"Education is a progressive discovery of our own ignorance."

—*Will "Fathead" Durant*

If I tried real hard, I might be able to remember more than a handful of events that happened in high school, but it would take a lot of concentration and my attention span on such matters is short. There was the water polo game I played in during my junior year where not only did the guy I was covering not score, but he only touched the ball three times. It was a complete and utter shutdown of their top scorer by a scrawny 110-pound weakling. But glory is fleeting. The game was knotted up at five-all at the end of regulation, and we all swam over to coach Radakovich for instructions for the overtime period.

"Okay, you guys," he said excitedly, "we're playing real tough. Is anybody tired?"

I thought for a moment. This was my first time in the pool in two weeks due to some un-Godly type fungus that had decided to attach itself to my underarm, and I was flat out exhausted. But then again, I had just played the game of my life, and I didn't want to come out. Finally, I figured I shouldn't be selfish, and for the good of the team, get a fresh body in there.

"Yeah, Coach ... I've had it," I said wearily dragging my sorry ass out of the water to the unanimous accolades of my teammates.

"Great game, Mitch," Brian Worth said slapping me on the back.

I sat down on the bench next to Rob and Don, my two best friends on the team who had already fouled out. Overtime started and not thirty seconds into it, the dude I had been guarding scored the winning goal and that was that. Brian turned and punched the slat fence behind us in anger and busted it up in the process.

Radakovich glared at me, his already red hair seemingly on fire and his blue eyes blazing a hole through my forehead, and screamed out loud enough for half the state's population to hear, "If you weren't such a damn picky eater Cox, you wouldn't have gotten tired and we would have won the damn game!"

I, along with Rob and Don, stared at him in disbelief. I played the best game I ever will or ever did play, and I'm blamed for the loss because this other moron couldn't cover the man. I grabbed my stuff and headed for the bus for what promised to be a long trip home.

By the time we got back to school, Coach had cooled his jets a bit and offered a brief apology for jumping all over my ass. But, unlike after every other game, he didn't offer me a ride home. My choice was clear. Do I ask Coach for a ride and risk more insults about my dietary habits, or do I call Dad and ask him to pick me up which, of course, would lead to voluminous stories about walking five miles a day in the snow to school (and of course, six miles back). I could never understand if a) roads back then were constructed differently, b) if all adults were just really stupid as kids, c) my dear father might actually be lying, or d) all of the above. I chose to ask Coach for the ride. And he gave me one just like always, but he didn't say a word the whole way home.

◆   ◆   ◆

My brother Kerry and me used to go down to Edwin's Pharmacy when we were kids and buy baseball cards almost every day. Back in the late 60s, you could get a pack of cards for a nickel. You'd get five cards and a stick of the worst chewing gum known to man. This stuff had so much sugar that one bite and you could kiss your saliva goodbye. It was like biting into a lemon with all the ensuing facial contortions. The gum usually cracked in the mouth, a sign of its freshness, and would lose its entire flavor by the time it became even remotely pliable. Our Dad would give us an allowance to spend with reckless abandon. I got a dime a week, and Kerry would get a quarter. Since he was only three years older than me, I never quite understood why he got 1½ times the allowance I got. Basic math dictated he should have received maybe 14 cents. Actually, it didn't really matter because Dad usually forgot to give us the money in the first place and Kerry and I were either too chicken or too stupid to remind him.

So there we'd sit on the corner of Burbank Blvd and Whitsett Avenue in North Hollywood ripping open packs, chewing this horrible gum and making our dentist happy. North Hollywood is really an odd name for this area of L.A. since it's a good 30 miles from Hollywood. My parents bought the house I grew up in back in 1961. At that time, it was a twenty-five year-old, two bedroom house with a big backyard filled with apricot, grapefruit, lemon and orange trees.

The front yard was a mixture of brush and palm and magnolia trees. My parents put in a swimming pool when they figured we were old enough and intelligent enough not to drown ourselves by accident. They ripped out all the brush and paved over the front yard in the form of a figure eight with two magnolias filling in the holes. This did not please the neighbors, whose front yards all looked like the ones on *Leave it to Beaver*. Mom and Dad didn't really care though. They've never been the kind to stand on one side of the fence while the neighbors relate the story of Aunt Sophie's bladder operation. They knew the parents of the kids we played with and that's about all.

In 1970, we moved to Westlake Village, one of the original pre-planned communities that have now spawned like horny salmon featuring street names like Freshwind, Fairbreeze, and Whitesail. It was, at the time, mostly open spaces with a few houses easily outnumbered by thousands of stately oak trees. Into the middle of all this flora and fauna they built a zillion homes and a lake.

My parents took Kerry and me out there in July of 1970 to look at what my Mom hoped would be our future return address. We were not exactly a tough sell. Throw a ten-year old kid and a fourteen-year old kid into an area with trees, hills, a lake, ducks, rabbits and God knows what else and the results are rather predictable. Just when Mom and Dad figured that we had reached a level of excitement not to be seen again, at least in my case, till nine years later when Janet Finnell took her clothes off in my dorm room, they set the proverbial hook.

"All right boys," Mom said, "we have a small problem. Dad and I would really love to move to this house, and we know you would too. But, we had also planned to pay for your college education when that time came. Unfortunately, we can't afford to do both. So … we leave it up to you. We can stay in North Hollywood, and we'll pay for your college, OR WE CAN MOVE OUT TO THIS BEAUTIFUL AREA AND YOU CAN PAY FOR YOUR OWN SCHOOLING. WHADDYA SAY?"

The emphasis, I admit, is mine, but that's how it sounded to my ears. Like I said though, it wasn't a tough sell. College? What's that?? The future? What's that?? We're talkin' ducks and rabbits and all sorts of fun stuff like that. It, in retrospect, was one of the great political snow jobs of our lifetime. Mom and Dad swept through the young and ignorant California delegation like a tornado through a mobile home park.

So now, the only hang-up was selling the house we lived in. My parents paid $19,000 for it back in 1960, so after adding the pool and all the other stuff, they decided to ask for $34,500. At the time, that was supposed to be a fairly unrealistic figure to shoot for, but my Mom always aimed to the high side. I don't remember much of what happened next except that all of the sudden, there were a hell of a lot of people traipsing through our living room. The next day the phone rang and my Mom started getting real excited.

"Right ... okay ... thank you ... goodbye," she said slamming the phone down and breaking into a full sprint around the house. "Bill, Bill!" she screamed looking for my Dad, "where are you?"

"I'm in the bathroom. Why, are we moving?"

"Yeah, so hurry up!"

Certain things in life are impossible. Hurrying up when you're doing a number one is one of them ...

"Bill, we have 30 days to get out! I just accepted an offer," Mom said, now starting to laugh hysterically.

Behind the bathroom door, Dad started to laugh too.

2

○ ○
"Only two things are infinite, the universe and human stupidity, and I'm not sure about the former."

—Albert "Fathead" Einstein

Seven years later, I'm pouring through every college catalog I can get my hands on trying to figure out what lucky school will be the recipient of my vast knowledge. I was expecting to receive a few offers though I'm not really sure why since both my grades and SAT scores were just a bit above average. For some ridiculous reason, I had my heart set on attending the University of Kentucky, for no other reason than the fact that I liked their basketball team. So I applied and was accepted. Now there was only one rather large problem, and that was tuition that ran upwards of $800 per quarter. No problem I thought—Kerry went away to school and while he did work his tail off, Mom and Dad still helped him with the financial end of things. I was sure they'd be thrilled to help their youngest.

"So what do you think guys, you cover the tuition and I'll take care of everything else?" I pleaded.

"Mitch, don't you remember what we discussed when we moved out here?" Mom replied.

"Yeah, but …"

"We said that if we moved out here we couldn't pay for your education."

"Yeah, but …"

"And you agreed to those terms."

"Yeah, but …"

I could see there was no way I was going to win this one, no matter how pathetic I attempted to look. So I relented and talked myself into attending Cal State Northridge, a university located a mere 30 miles away from home.

My supposed intellectual strengths lie in the "liberal arts" like communications, English, etc. Not science in any way, shape or form. Dissecting animals that have been soaking in formaldehyde was never my idea of a great time, so I

7

didn't approach my first and only year of college biology with a large amount of enthusiasm.

The class, Biology 101, was held in Sierra Hall, a nine-story white stucco job in the middle of campus a stone's throw away from the library. It was widely rumored that there were all sorts of dead bodies stored under the library in a secret area, the results of unsuccessful scientific experiments. So anyway, I'm sitting in a class full of fifty strangers, all of us freshmen, all of us scared shitless that this class would be the toughest thing we ever hoped to live through. My only hope was that our professor wouldn't be named Herbert or some other scientific geek name. Suddenly, the door flew open and this guy bounced in walking like one leg was shorter than the other, eyes glued to the floor, carrying a ton of books, but as of yet, no dead animals. He tossed the load of books onto the old wood desk in the front of the class and scrawled his name on the blackboard. For the life of me, I can't recall this guy's name so for lack of anything better, I'll call him Fred. So Fred wrote his name and the name of the course on the board and began to call roll. At this point, this guy had still not established any sort of eye contact with the class. And he never did for the rest of the hour. The next time class met, the same pattern was followed: Fred bops in, Fred throws books on desk, Fred turns to chalkboard and starts writing biology type stuff. But he never looked at us! I felt sorry for the dude ahead of me because he had a question for two straight days and couldn't get Fred to call on him.

"Question!" the guy finally yelled out.

"Go ahead," said Fred, with his back still to the class.

So this guy asked his question, which for now is irrelevant, but that's how things went for at least the first three weeks. Finally, some of us got together at lunch one day and set up a pool on how long it would take before Fred would look at us, and when he did, what he would look like.

"I think he's probably just shy," said this girl named Monica or Marlene or something like that. I've never been too good with names.

"The guy's a nut," said this dude named Jeff. "He probably looks like Manson or some other psycho."

After all was said and done, we agreed Fred had to look at us before the midterm and that he was a cross between the Broadway actor, Robert Morse, and the Elephant Man. Damn if we didn't nail that puppy on the head! About three or four class sessions later, the inevitable happened.

"Question!" a blonde across the room yelled, her arm stiff with rigor mortis.

"Go ahead," Fred answered, face to the blackboard.

"Is the mid-term going to cover everything we've learned so far?" she asked.

Why is there always someone this stupid in every class?

Apparently, Fred also found this question rather absurd. He wheeled around, cocked his head to the right and looked up at the bimbo. His face certainly wasn't frightening, but he squinted so much the wrinkles went all the way down to his chin.

So now the suspense was over. By the time finals rolled around, Fred was our buddy. It was a cold December day, or at least as cold as it gets in L.A. We're all in class waiting for Fred to come and give us our final. Jeff is there, along with Monica or Marlene (whatever), and the blonde bimbo, who is still in a state of disbelief over the fact that yes, indeed, the final covers everything we've learned so far. The door swung open and in walked Fred. In one hand, he's got a huge stack of papers—in the other, a tennis ball. And he's wearing a Dodgers cap that's two sizes too small. Incredibly dignified.

"Take one and pass the rest of the person behind you," he said. What a brilliant concept. I had taken tests for God knows how long and this was always the easiest part.

Silence enveloped the room as we all worked hard trying to figure out if amoebas have lips or some kind of trash.

THUMP!

Question #10: In a macrobiotic synthesis, describe the co-relation ...

THUMP!

Okay ... let's see ... macrobiotic synthesis ...

THUMP!

... describe the reaction ...

THUMP!

... I mean co-relation ...

THUMP!

... if the synthesis ... THUMP! *...* what the hell?

I finally looked up to see Fred sitting in his old wooden chair, leaning back with his feet resting on the metal thing that holds the chalk under the board. From this position, he's bouncing the tennis ball off the wall, thereby explaining the annoying THUMP, THUMP sound.

"Excuse me, do you think you could cool it with the tennis ball?" I asked.

"Right," said Fred, pausing only to swing around to face the heathen that broke up his playtime. "You don't like baseball?"

"I love it," I replied, "but not during my biology final."

Fred pondered that one for a moment, tugged his hat as far down his wrinkly face as he could and swung back around. For a few moments, everyone was still either looking at me or Fred. Then the rustling of paper and such began, and everyone, including myself, returned to the matter at hand.

Question #10: In a macrobiotic synthesis, describe the co-relation of both the …
THUMP!

3

"Those who cannot remember the past, are condemned to a lousy grade"

—*George "Fathead" Santayana*

I can't sing, or dance. I can't play a musical instrument, though I studied the clarinet for three years—which kind of sounds like for three years straight I sat staring intently at it. I tried guitar, but when I couldn't even play a reasonable rendition of "Layla" within the first couple months, I quit. Patience is not one of my virtues. I also can't play soccer, run a mile in under six minutes, or eat fried squid. But I can bullshit. I was the Lord King Bullshitter in high school and the teachers would eat it up. So when I arrived at the friendly confines of CSUN, I just assumed that the professors there would open up and say "AAAhhhhh." I also thought Mondale was a cinch in '84.

In order to satisfy some sort of American duty, incoming freshmen were required to take a history class dealing with our country, pre or post 1865. Pre-1865 sounded rather boring to me, so I chose the latter under the assumption (wrong again) that we would cruise through the late 1800s, get into World War I, the Depression, Hitler and the other sickos, then Vietnam and the whole 60s-70s era that I could relate to. I also assumed Dukakis would beat Bush in '88.

Stephen Wright was the head honcho of the class. At first sight, it was obvious that no one had clued this guy into the fact that this was 1978 and people didn't wear their hair in the old "Hi, I just got out of the Marines" look. Mr. Wright, for all his dorky looks—the glasses, the pens in the pocket, the whole nerd 101 style—was the smartest professor I had over the rest of my college days. The man had written three or four books on Chinese history, two or three on European immigration and lectured throughout the country. He was truly a brilliant man with the personality of a turnip. But most of all, despite his obvious intellect, this man possessed the best set of olfactory nerves in the Western Hemisphere. He could smell the BS coming before it hit the paper. Unfortunately, I didn't learn this very important lesson until mid-term time.

The first half of the semester was spent entirely on European immigration. By mid-March, I was up to my ears in stories about some family of Greek yahoos who, with thirty six cents in their pocket, arrived at Ellis Island only to turn their pocket change into the proverbial American dream. Now it's not that I didn't find these stories utterly fascinating, and, like castor oil, a small amount might have been digestible. But to sit in class for an hour-and-a-half, then have to go home and read about it, not to mention working six hours a day, well, it all got rather tedious. So much so that most nights I fell asleep while reading page twelve of *Foreign Dudes 1, USA 0* or whatever the hell the book was called. So the mid-term arrived, and there is but one question on the whole test. It looked something like this:

"Using actual events and personalities as examples, describe the effect that European immigrants had on our country, and the way they in turn were affected."

Great. I stared into my hand as it covered my eyes hoping that at some point, I used incredible foresight and scribbled the answer on my index finger. Wrong again. "Fear not Cox ol' boy, you've been in tougher spots than this," I thought. "Just pull out the shovel and start working." And that I did. Four pages of some of my finest intellectual gibberish. I used examples, never too specific of course, to describe the initial shock suffered by the immigrants, the partitioning off into neighborhoods of ethnic origins that still exist today, facts, details, insight … bullshit.

And he saw right through it. Mr. Wright held his nose and turned what I thought was a pretty damn fine piece of work into a D+.

"Mr. Wright?," I said, figuring it couldn't hurt to toss another shovelful out there, "I think you might have made a mistake on my exam."

"What's your name?"

"Cox."

"No mistake."

4

"Traveling there was really boring so I headed for the ditch. It was a rough ride, but I met more interesting people there."

—*Neil "Fathead" Young*

The main student parking lot at Cal State Northridge is about the size of Rhode Island. It is an endless row of evenly spaced white lines, three foot concrete pillars and overhead lights. The only thing that disrupts the beauty is an occasional cement oval encircling a sickly looking tree.

The campus itself is a small city serving over 30,000 people. The sounds like a bad ad for McDonalds, but you get the point. It's large. So large that it was virtually impossible to get to know anyone other than on a casual basis. Not that the size of the school was the only hold-up, in fact, that was a small reason. The big problem was that almost everyone commuted to the school, so it was like working for some huge corporation, except that no one wore stupid name tags and fresh coffee wasn't served in the lobby.

My brother Kerry had gone away to some Podunk place called Corvallis to attend Oregon State. At Oregon State, my brother drank, partied, got laid, drank some more, partied some more, got laid some more and even went to class now and then. He would come home during break and tell me all the fun and exciting things that were happening there, and all I could think about was how I couldn't wait to get to college.

So by the middle of my second semester at CSUN, I knew that something was missing. This was not what my brother had described to me. I wasn't drinking, I wasn't partying, and God knows I certainly wasn't getting laid. It was time to grow up and make a decision about what I wanted to do with my life. I wanted to get away to a new area, but I had to stay in California to keep it affordable. The UC system was out due to the fact that one of their entrance requirements was two years of high school level foreign language. I had none. I did take Spanish in sixth grade and got an "A" but the only phrases I retained were "Como estas?," "muy bien!," and "y no comprende', para mi arroz con pollo," which roughly means, "I don't understand, bring me the chicken and rice." Three top-notch phrases, but not nearly enough to impress the big wigs at Berkeley.

That left me with basically the rest of the California State University system. Anything around the L.A. area was eliminated for the reason that Mom would want me to visit on weekends, thus nullifying one of the reasons for going away in the first place. So that basically left Sacramento State, Fresno State, San Diego State, Humboldt State, San Francisco State and Chico State. Sacramento, Fresno, San Diego and San Francisco were never really in the running because of their central city location and similarities to Northridge, and from what I understood at the time, the women at Humboldt State resembled small musk ox. That left Chico State, a relatively small campus boasting an enrollment of more women than men among other fine aspects.

◆   ◆   ◆

On August 23, 1978, I jammed into the trunk of my blue Mazda RX-2 all of my worldly goods, minus the baseball cards my brother and I bought the decade before. Kerry was going to accompany me, on what turned out to be exactly 500 miles from doorstep to dorm room. We took off about eleven in the morning after a long tearful sayonara from Mom and a firm handshake from Dad.

"You guys drive carefully, and call us to let us know you made it okay," Dad instructed. This was his favorite sentence to use whenever Kerry or I went anywhere, even to the corner store. Mom, on the other hand, was not entirely thrilled with the prospect of her youngest living so far away in a town she never heard of. As far as she's concerned, if it's not located in the immediate Los Angeles metropolitan area, it might as well not exist. And when I told her I was going to Chico, she asked what a "Chico" was.

"Wasn't he one of those guys you like?"

"The Marx Brothers?"

"Yes, the Marx Brothers," she said.

"Well, yeah, Chico was one of the Marx Brothers," I explained, "but that's not who the University was named after."

"Who is it named after?"

"I don't know …"

"Well," she said, looking a bit disgusted, "I don't understand why you insist on going to a school so far away from home … especially when you don't know who it was named after."

Suddenly, I had a terrible thought. What if after getting up there, I found out that the school *was* indeed named after Chico Marx! Mom would be right, I would be wrong, and my diploma would seem rather silly.

It was too damn early in the morning for this was my only thought. I had eight to ten hours of driving ahead of me and all of this seemed rather absurd. I gave her a big hug, told her I loved her, and grabbed Kerry to leave.

We piled into the RX-2, which I had renamed Marvin "The Human Eraser" J. Mazda III for no particular reason, and headed out on Highway 101. As we drove past the brush covered hills of Agoura on our way into the valley, the enormity of what I was doing finally sunk in. This was it—the big move. I had already flushed four hundred dollars into a place to live which I had never seen, in a town I'd never been to, to live with a guy I'd never met. Drug addicts, they're probably all drug addicts, I thought. Insecurity was setting in like cement overshoes.

"What am I doing?" I muttered to myself.

"What's the problem?" asked Kerry.

"I can't believe what I'm doing here," I babbled. "I don't know a single person up there. I don't know anything about what's up there. I ... I ... what about Dodger games? Angel games? Or the Lakers?"

"You never went to a Lakers game in your life."

"That doesn't matter. I could have if I wanted to. That's not the point," I whined.

"Nothing to be scared about, Poo," Kerry said using an old nickname from our North Hollywood days, "everybody's basically in the same boat as you."

I hated it when he called me Poo. It has nothing to do with Winnie the Pooh or anything cute like that. It came about one day when I was seven or eight and I was over Jim Blanchard's house. Jim was my best friend growing up even though he used to beat the snot out of me occasionally, but that's the price of friendship, I guess. Anyway, he had two older brothers, Rick and Bob, who later became very successful as lawyers, which in most cases is as big an insult as I can think of. So it's Bob's senior prom or homecoming or something, and I'm over playing with Jim when Bob comes out of his room buttoning up a white ruffled dress shirt. As soon as he saw me, he started chasing me around the house squealing, "Ooooo, Mitchiepoo, I just love boys!"

It stuck.

Variations on "Mitchiepoo" followed including, in no particular order: Poostick, Pooface, Poosie, and the overall most popular, plain old "Poo." No matter—I hated them all.

The San Diego Freeway runs through the valley like an eight-lane steamroller, crushing anything in its way including whatever peace and quiet the locals may have ever enjoyed. As the Human Eraser rolled through the city of Northridge, I could see the top few floors of Sierra Hall on the CSUN campus, and the state flag waving goodbye to me. In front of us lay a ton of mountains and a truck killing stretch of road known as the Grapevine. Actually, Grapevine is a tiny truck stop at the bottom of the mountain on the north side featuring the standard assortment of gas stations and cheesy restaurants. But no homes. I never could figure out where the people that worked there lived. Maybe they all get transported like cattle every day by a northbound truck and returned home later in the day.

The ascent up the Grapevine was long and tedious, especially for the Human Eraser who wasn't quite used to hauling such a load. The Grapevine tops out at Tejon Pass at a little over four thousand feet, and it's hard to believe that with all the beauty of the mountains and trees surrounding you, that you left the second largest city in the U.S. a little over an hour ago.

As the Human Eraser's temperature gauge reached the upper levels, we hit the Tejon Pass and as the old saying goes, it was all downhill from there. Kerry had taken the wheel when we first left home, and had spent the majority of the first couple hours on the road drinking Bud and cursing out other drivers. However, now he was happy because the uphill climb had slowed us down to forty-five miles per hour and his patience was wearing thin.

"Now, let's see what this piece of shit can do," he growled.

Kerry dropped it into neutral and let the momentum carry us to new heights of being scared shitless. We whizzed by semi's and Chevys and everything else like they were parked for the view. The trees blurred at white knuckle speed and it suddenly dawned on me that my life was going to end in a flaming ball of twisted metal near some town called Gorman, home of a Chevron station and a fleabag hotel with half its sign missing.

"Slow down, Kerr," I whimpered.

"Total control, Poo, total control," he assured me. God, I hated it when he called me that.

The end of the Grapevine has a spectacular view of the lower San Joaquin Valley which on a winter day would most likely be covered in tule fog. But this was summer so things were different. Instead, it was covered with a thick layer of smoke, smog and other floating crud held down by the invisible lid of an inversion layer.

"I thought only L.A. looked like that," Kerry said.

It was like entering a brown ocean, but not getting wet. I figured if Kerry's driving didn't kill me, the lack of oxygen in the valley would.

We made it to the bottom of the hill and the bustling metropolis of Grape-vine. We let the Human Eraser take a breather while we ate some of Denny's finest cuisine. For as long as I live, I will never understand how that restaurant has stayed in business. The food tastes like wet cardboard, the atmosphere is stifling and stale, and let's face it, most of the waitresses could double as circus animals. What keeps Denny's in business, I suppose, are morons like Kerry and me who are too stupid to think ahead and pack a lunch.

◆   ◆   ◆

Buttonwillow, Kettleman City, Santa Nella, Los Banos. The excitement was getting to be too much. Would it have really killed the highway construction department to put a curve on Interstate 5 at some point? I was being hypnotized by the little white lines on the pavement, and the thrill-packed scenery that surrounded us. Meanwhile, Kerry was on his fourth or fifth Bud and, except for changing the tape every forty minutes or so, had hardly moved. It was about a thousand degrees in the valley, and I didn't have air conditioning. Well, at least not in a realistic sense. The Eraser was equipped with air conditioning, but when I bought my car stereo and could find no other place to install it because of its rather large size, my friend suggested we attach it to the air conditioning unit.

"No problem," Chris said, "we'll just drill three holes into the plastic casing and that'll be strong enough to hold it."

It almost worked. The first screw went in just as he said it would. So did the second. The third one, though, cracked the Freon pipe and all this cold yellow shit started spraying all over the place. Ever since then, the air conditioner would only make this sickly groaning noise when it was turned on. So basically, I broke a four hundred dollar A/C system to install a one hundred dollar stereo. A brilliant financing move. But, at least we had the tunes.

According to the signs, we were still one hundred-and-sixty miles from Sacramento which was ten miles closer than we were at the last sign. Since the Highway 99/I-5 split back near Grapevine, these dumb-ass signs are up informing you that you have a zillion miles to your destination, which is no big deal if you're headed five miles or so, but the first sign we saw said:

SAN FRANCISCO	**291**
SACRAMENTO	**290**

So we watched the odometer tick off a mile and in between wiping sweat away, we'd say, "Shit, only two hundred and eighty-nine more miles to go, piece of cake." But each mile took progressively longer as the drive wore on. After a while, my body was bitching at me like an ex-wife. My back was sticking to the seat, my butt was asleep and my legs were cramping up. Plus, I needed to piss like a Russian racehorse. Then we came upon another sign:

NEXT REST STOP   **35 MILES**

What I wouldn't have done for a Denny's at that point.

Several hours later, we finally reached Sacramento. It was there that we experienced the thrill and excitement of changing highways. We merged onto Highway 99 and drove another one hundred miles going through towns like Yuba City, Live Oak, Gridley, and Biggs. But then, finally, the sign we were waiting for arrived:

CHICO
NEXT 9 EXITS

Goodbye, L.A. Goodbye, Kentucky. Goodbye, Northridge.
Hello, Chico.

5

"God is my roommate"

—*Fathead*

By the time the Human Eraser escorted us down First Avenue in Chico, it was pitch black, which was kind of a drag since I was rather anxious to see what the town looked like. We followed the signs that supposedly would lead us to the bastion of higher learning, but it soon became apparent to us that we missed a turn somewhere along the line. After driving around in circles for what seemed like an eternity, going over and over the same set of railroad tracks, I finally suggested we ask a friendly passerby where the hell the damn school was.

"Excuse us," I said, rolling down the window, "could you tell us where the college is?"

A gentleman sporting a ponytail and a tie-dye shirt pointed to a building less than one hundred feet away. "See that?"

"Yeeaaahhh …"

"That's it."

"Thank you very much," I said meekly, rolling the window back up. "We knew that."

Kerry whipped around the corner, found a parking space, and in the warm darkness, we went in search of my new living accommodations. When I filled out the preference forms for dorm space, I had requested that I be placed in Shasta Hall for no other reason than I liked the name. The other two dorms were also named after mountains; Lassen and Whitney. Lassen Hall turned out to be an exact replica of Shasta, a three-story brick contraption with all the charm of a SS guard. Whitney, on the other hand, was a nine story building known throughout as "the Zoo." The name derived from the fact that Whitney housed over five hundred hormone-dripping, loudmouth eighteen-to-nineteen year-old kids crammed into rooms the size of a Rubik's Cube.

Shasta Hall, as was the case with Lassen, was designed by the same guy who designed San Quentin, or at least that was the rumor. Inside, it was fairly ordinary looking. White walls, kind of a puke green carpet, and in the lobby, a couple of easy chairs that you might find on a visit to your grandmother's house. Kerry and me made our way to the front desk and were shown to what would be my home sweet home for the next nine months. Room 110, third door on the right, first floor, east side. The description was bigger than the room.

"Your roommate has already arrived," the young lady who took us to the room said. She pointed at these two pieces of construction paper taped to the door. On one was my name, and on the other, my new roommate.

"Dave, what?" I said, not having any idea how to pronounce this guy's last name.

"It's pronounced 'Korea' like the country, it's just spelled C-O-R-R-E-I-A."

"Is he oriental?" I asked.

Kerry and the woman both looked at me.

"Is he?" I repeated.

"I'm not really his brother," Kerry informed her.

"Good thing," she said walking away.

Kerry grabbed his bag with his left hand and shook my hand with his right. "Well Poo, this is it. Just don't say any more dumbass things and you'll be fine." And with that bit of brotherly advice, he was gone in search of a hotel room.

◆   ◆   ◆

I walked down the hallway in search of a bathroom. I'd had to piss since Sacramento, and that was a good two hours ago. The hallway walls were large brick with about fourteen coats of white paint, and the carpet was the same puke green as in the lobby. The bathroom was located on the left side of the hall, directly at the mid-point of the rooms. There was a guy washing his face, groaning every time he brought the rag up. He glanced at me and kind of grunted a hello or something.

"How you doing?" My typical response.

After taking care of business, I went back to the room and sat on the bed, attempting to take in all the trappings of my palatial suite My new roommate's stuff was all over the joint and it got me wondering who this guy was and what he was like. There were clothes strewn everywhere, Frisbees, a primo ten-speed, and of course, the stereo. Not much in terms of clues. There was also a red plastic thing that was absolutely gross looking. At the time, I had no idea what it was used for, but in time, my naiveté in the world of drug paraphernalia would diminish.

All in all, there wasn't much. Two beds, two dressers, two closets, two mirrors, two shelving units ... it was like being on Noah's Ark. Our room's window faced out towards Lassen Hall and the grass area that separated the two buildings. On either side of the window was the shelving unit and underneath that, the tan metal desk. The beds were Army cot style, metal bracing with wire and a four inch mattress thrown on top. No box spring. Great for my back, I thought. So, there I was, wondering what the hell I was doing in this God forsaken place when the dude from the bathroom walked in.

"Hey," he grunted throwing shit on his bed in a thousand different directions.

"Hey," I said. This is my new roommate. This is the guy I have to live with for the next nine months in a space no bigger than a medicine cabinet.

"What's your name?" he asked in between throwing shit back and forth.

"Mitch. You're Dave, right?"

"Yeah, right," he smiled, kind of. Finally, he sat down on his bed, and looked at me with slits where his eyes should have been.

"You sick?" I asked.

"No, why?"

"Your eyes don't look so good. They're kind of red. I just thought maybe you were sick or something."

Hello Dave, meet Mr. Naïve.

He shook his head. "You a freshman?" he asked.

"No, sophomore," and I briefly gave him the rundown on my fascinating life and fun-filled experience at Northridge.

"This is my second year in this shithole," he said. "A buddy of mine named Stu and I were gonna get an apartment, but he fucked around for so long that I had to come back here. This is even the same damn room I had last year."

"Kind of a drag, huh?"

"Wait'll you taste the food," he laughed. Maybe, I thought, this guy was going to be okay. "I'll see you later," he said, getting up and walking out the door. I didn't see him again for about a week. He was so bummed about being back in the dorms that he went out and got so blasted and high that he just crashed wherever he was at the time.

I didn't really have the time to worry about where he was during that lost week because I had about a million things to do. There was registering for classes, a process where they took eighty thousand students and stuck them in Acker Gym on the hottest day of the year and watched them run over each other in a vain attempt to sign up for their selected classes. Of course, the non-aggressive among us ended up looking like abused puppies when the professor teaching the class we desperately needed told us that it's full "but I'll put you on the waiting list."

"How many are ahead of me?"

"Well, let's see … 1 … 2 … 3 … 4"

"Four?"

"Thousand …"

"Oh."

So you end up with a schedule featuring classes like:

Accounting 105—A class designed for students not majoring in Business, Accounting, Economics or any other discipline where a working brain cell might come in handy. Class discussion will focus on the history of number systems, how numbers have benefited mankind, and the future of numbers. Students lapsing into a deep coma during class will receive half credit.

And so on …

Besides registration, I was spending a lot of time trying like hell to find a store to buy all the shit I forgot at home. Not to mention that my birthday arrived two days after I did. It was one hundred million degrees in the shade, and for all intents and purposes, I didn't know a soul in town. The first week or two, your roommate is your closest friend because you're trying to get to know people and since you're living with him, that's the logical place to start. Since my roomie was out in who knows what gutter keeping the South American drug cartel in Italian suits and Rolls Royce's, I spent the night of Thursday, August 25, 1978 in sweltering brick box #110 watching a spider walk across my wall in a never-ending quest to land one of its spindly little legs on my favorite Cheryl Tiegs poster. Just before the little bastard could make contact though, I'd give it a spritz of antiperspirant which would really piss him off. This went on for awhile until the poor little guy's legs curled up for the last time and he fell to the floor in a crumpled heap of dead spider. That ended my birthday party.

◆   ◆   ◆

By the end of September, things had started to develop a routine. Dave was back from the Hinterland, and for the most part, we got along okay. He hated my music, and I his, but other than an occasional obscenity hurled, we were buds. Also, by this time, I had gotten to know the rest of the guys on the wing. This was truly the oddest assortment of characters ever placed together in a controlled living environment short of San Quentin. Some I got to know better than others, of course, but that didn't matter. We were First East, or as we later became known, "Freaks." And there was sort of a perverse pride we took in knowing that there was something about us that distinguished us from the other wings.

If this were still high school, we would have separated into our various cliques; the stoners, the jocks, the brains ... okay, maybe not the "brains"—and never have spoken a word to each other. But this miscast group of hermits, drug abusers, Christians and the socially awkward were now a family. One certainly you wouldn't want to invite to any special occasion, but a family nonetheless.

6

○ ○
"On Halloween, the parents sent their kids out looking like me."

—*Rodney "Fathead" Dangerfield*

I have never been a big fan of Halloween. Celebrating death by dressing up as skeletons, witches and the like, always seemed a rather odd thing to do, not to mention giving candy coated rewards to little pipsqueaks who scream "TRICK OR TREAT!" as if you've got a choice. So when the end of October rolled around, and the "Freaks" were informed that it was our civic duty to create a "haunted wing," I was less than enthused. So was everyone else.

"Please, you guys," Big John, our resident advisor begged us, "just do me this one favor? It's an important community outreach type thing."

He had already asked us at least ten times for just "one favor" in the first two months, but we were pushovers for a guy six-foot-five and about three hundred pounds. Talking to Big John was always a challenge: first, because he was so damn big, and second, because he had one eye akimbo. You couldn't look him straight in the eyes, because while one eye might be looking at you, his other eye was somewhere out in left field. I always felt like I was boxing him instead of talking to him because I spent most of the time bobbing and weaving trying to figure out which eye he was using.

Steve Feldman, our stereotypical Jew from 114, asked why we needed to create a haunted wing.

"It's done every year for the local elementary school kids," said Big John. "Goodness, we had a great one last year, remember, Dave? The kids loved it!"

"The kids thought it sucked," Dave replied. What a great roomie.

"So what are we supposed to do?" I asked.

"Just create a kind of haunted house atmosphere. I mean it should be scary, but not too scary. After all, these are just little kids."

"I say we scare the fuck out of the little bastards," said Crazy Al.

"NO, that's not the point of this you guys!" Big John exclaimed, his right eye getting really big and his left eye checking out a cheeseburger someone left on the table. "It's supposed to still be fun! And they still get candy at the end."

Big John was having a tough time winning us over. This was not the most community-minded group of guys in the world. Crazy Al from 120 was into it, but for all the wrong reasons. What a funky dude he was. "Crazy" Al Lieberman was a stocky little Jewish guy, as strong as an ox, and as level-headed as Charles Manson. When he was a kid, he got his left leg caught in a mower or something and had to get it amputated just above the knee. I found this out the hard way one day when I saw him walking down the hall on crutches, wearing just a bath-robe. At a distance, from behind, I thought he had hurt his leg and was just hold-ing it up.

"Hey, Al," I innocently yelled down the white hallway with the puke green carpet, "What happened to your leg?"

He turned around, and I could feel his crazy blue eyes staring at me. He undid his robe so I could get the whole picture. "I don't know, Cox, where the fuck did you hide it?"

Mr. Foot, meet Mr. Mouth.

Crazy Al, for all of his insanity, was genius enough, however, to come up with a brilliant scheme. Despite having just the one leg, he was still an excellent skier. Al would contact all of the major ski manufacturers and tell them his story and out of sympathy and positive public relations, the company would respond with free skis. Al, in turn, would then pair up the skis he didn't need and sell them. And then buy beer.

So anyway, a compromise was reached with Big John, in which he agreed not to bother us about the haunted wing idea again, and we promised we wouldn't scare the total shit out of the kids. We also agreed amongst ourselves that none of us really wanted to put much of an effort into this whole affair.

Halloween Day was the first day that I was able to experience yet another val-ley phenomenon. When I woke up and peered out between the Levelors, it looked like the way London is portrayed on TV. What appeared to be fog was so thick, I couldn't even see Lassen Hall just a couple hundred or so feet away. But this wasn't white and misty, but rather gray and soupy looking. I threw on some clothes and ventured bravely outside. As soon as I got out the door and took my first breath, my lungs started burning and I began to cough like an emphysema patient. Through stinging eyes, I could tell there was no one else stupid enough to be outside in this shit.

"What the hell is going on out there?" I coughed to the girl behind the front desk after I stumbled back inside.

"It's burning season. Isn't it terrible?"

I looked back outside through the big glass doors. "What are they burning, downtown?"

"No," she laughed, "the rice fields. Every fall, the farmers burn their rice fields."

"Why?"

"I don't know."

Obviously, not an Ag major I thought.

"So what are we supposed to do when it's like this?"

"Well ... most everyone stays indoors. Or goes to the library to study."

Now I can't stand staying indoors doing nothing. I must have run into a thousand guys who can plop their asses down in an easy chair, with a sixer of Bud by their side and watch football games till their eyes bleed. And going to the library? To study? Out of the question.

I went back to my cellblock muttering how this was so much bullshit, grabbed my Frisbee and sat out in the lobby in one of those grandma-style chairs. I waited for close to half-an-hour until someone I kind of knew came out looking bored to death. Enter the newest psycho on the block, a guy named David Ghorenzidelli, or as we ended up calling him, David G. because no one could figure out how to say his last name.

David G. lived upstairs on Second West where all the lunatics lived. Actually, my wing is where the real lunatics were, but these guys were a different sort from us. While our wing was filled with lots of weird guys, Second West was a breeding ground for former high school football players, and any other asshole who thought that not only was he God's gift to womankind, but humanity itself. Loud, obnoxious ... guys who yell "PARTY!" first thing in the morning, and are surprised to learn that they have to attend an occasional class now and then in order to continue enjoying all that university life has to offer. David G., to his everlasting credit, didn't fit into that mold. Unfortunately, he didn't quite fit into any mold. Rumor had it that his mom or sister or both died in a car accident and that he never really quite got over it. His facial expression would rarely change; his lips tightly pursed behind a full dark beard and moustache. But it was those eyes, I guess, that gave me the heebie-jeebies. They could burn right through you like a laser one minute, then look glazed over and expressionless the next.

But all that shit didn't matter now, because he was here and I was bored.

"David G., my main man!" I said rising to my feet, "you want to go throw the Fris for awhile?"

"Sure," he said, with all the warmth of an asparagus spear. Little did I know then that this nut cake would be one of my roommates the next year.

So to make a long story longer, we went out and chucked the Fris for awhile before both contracting lung cancer and dying a slow, painful death. Actually, the only reason the story about the smoke is evenly remotely important is for what it did to my vocal cords. The smoke caused me to spend the rest of the day coughing my brains out, so that by the end of the evening, I sounded like Broderick Crawford on valium.

Meanwhile, the Freaks were hard at work creating the proverbial haunted wing.

"This is shit," my dear roomie Dave was quick to offer.

"Fuck you," said Jim, a big red-haired kid from some little town near the Oregon border. Jim wasn't especially weird or anything, he was just a guy who drank a lot of beer, smoked a lot of dope, and liked to use the word "fuck" or variations thereof at least once in every sentence. He could have easily lived on Second West, but we got him instead.

Dave was right. The whole set-up revolved around the side door where the kids would enter the dorm. At that point, all the lights would be off, and the kids would step onto mattresses that were thrown on the floor. This was designed not to scare them, but mostly to make them lose their balance. While the kids would be stumbling around a bit, about five or six guys would stand there with pillows and as Crazy Al so delicately put it, "beat the shit out of the little bastards." At the same time this was happening, I was supposed to make scary noises into a mike we had hooked up to Dave's stereo. That was the whole show.

"Guys," said Feldman, rubbing his belly habitually, "this isn't scary. It's supposed to be scary."

"So what do you fuckin' want to do?" asked Jim, using his most polite manners.

"Why don't we just shine a bright light on Al, that'll scare the shit out of 'em," Dave offered.

"What do we do with them after they've been beaten?" I asked.

Everyone kind of looked at one another hoping that between them, an idea might come. No soap.

Finally, Feldman offered to put his curly head to it and waddled off to his room to get high.

"Maybe fucked up I'll be able to think of something," he said.

There was the idea everyone was waiting for. We all piled into cellblock 114 and shortly thereafter, drugs were being set on fire.

"Where's Greg?" I asked, referring to Feldman's roommate, a real normal guy on the outside, but on the inside, someone you read about in the paper as a guy who "kept to himself" right before he blows away his whole neighborhood. He wasn't violent or anything, the guy rarely lost his temper. He was just confused. Like a lot of people with a strong religious upbringing, there seemed to be two sides to him. The outside was this clean cut, hair never over the ears, accounting major who loved his family and attended church on Sunday. On the inside though, was this guy just dying to get out and have a good time. He bought an acoustic guitar but would only try and play music that not only required, but demanded, an electric sound. Shit like Hendrix, Skynard, the Stones. He'd call me into his room to play something he'd just figured out, and after awhile, I knew what to expect. "Purple Haze" just doesn't make it on an acoustic.

So anyway, Greg was hitting the library as usual and everyone else was getting shitfaced. Except me.

"C'mon Mitch, just put your fuckin' mouth here and suck," said Jim handing me a bong that I think was a clear yellow at one time. I was sitting in the corner listening to Eric Clapton's "Layla" on some headphones and just watching the guys. I stared at the thing for a minute, trying to figure out what in hell scared me so much about the whole thing. Was I afraid it would burn the shit out of my lungs, or that I'd like the stuff too much? I wasn't sure. Maybe a bong that got cleaned once every five or six years might have helped persuade me to take a hit, but not this time. Instead, I politely declined, put the headphones back on and rejoined Clapton just in time for the finale.

The room was absolutely filled with smoke. Gerald took a big hit, and then said he had to go pee and to open the door when he gave us the secret knock.

"I'll knock once, then twice, then three times. That's the secret knock. OK?" he explained.

There was a general murmur of agreement, but with the headphones on, I couldn't tell if anyone had really understood what Gerald had said.

A few seconds later, Kevin heard a knock on the door. He took a really big hit, and then opened it up. But instead of Gerald's friendly mug, we were met with the evil eyes of Big John. Well, okay, one part of the room was met by one eye, and the other part was met by the other eye. But the point is that Big John wasn't Gerald, Big John wasn't happy, and Kevin really needed to exhale in the worst way.

Big John stepped through the doorway and closed the door behind him. He had a sullen, disappointed look on his face as he stared at his young charges. At this point, Kevin could no longer hold his breath and proceeded to blast out a cloud of marijuana smoke that would have made Bob Marley proud. Of course, knowing the seriousness of the situation, we all did the only logical thing we could do.

We cracked up.

Then, without warning, a knock on the door. Then two knocks. Then three knocks. Big John opened the door and after pissing in his pants, Gerald slowly popped his head through the tiny opening.

"Gerald, I don't think you want to be in here right now," said Big John in a deeply serious voice.

Gerald quickly managed to put his two remaining working brain cells together and figured out that his timing couldn't be more exquisite. A small grin creased his face as he agreed with Big John that this den of scoundrels was no place for him.

"Hey, mmm … wait a minute … mmm … that's, uh … mmm … bullshit," mumbled Kevin, his eyes a mere pair of slits on his face.

"You guys, this is unacceptable," said Big John. "I'm going to have to write each of you up for this."

"Mmmm … what does that … mmm … uh, mean … mmm, exactly when … mmm … you say you have … mmm … to write us up?" Kevin said while desperately trying to maintain his balance.

"I will be writing each of you up for possession of marijuana," replied Big John. "We don't call the cops, but if you are caught again, you will be kicked out of the dorms."

Suddenly, the seriousness of the situation hit me.

"Hey, John, I wasn't doing anything. I was just listening to music," I protested. Everyone agreed, trying to help out by adding that I was too much of a pussy to get high. I would have been okay with just a simple nod of agreement.

"Sorry, but you're in the room and that means you're as guilty as they are," said Big John. With that, he turned and stormed out.

Not a second later, Gerald returned to the room. "What the hell happened?" he asked.

"Hmmm … we got fucked … mmm," Kevin said. "I think I need to get high."

An hour or so later, Crazy Al got up and staggered over to the door saying he had "a great idea. A real fucking great idea!"

"Get some more beer!" Feldman yelled.

"BEER!" everyone screamed.

Crazy Al slowly turned around, raised his eyebrows like Jack Nicholson and whispered, "More beer?"

"MORE BEER!!" Gosh, what an outstanding group of individuals I was involved with.

◆   ◆   ◆

We didn't see Crazy Al till about six that evening when he came back with this shit-eatin' grin on his face still harping about his "fucking great idea." The rest of us were busy trying to clear our heads and get ready for the kids to come through our haunted wing. We took about six mattresses and threw 'em on the floor. Feldman came up with the idea of hanging string from the ceiling so it would feel like they were walking through spider webs or something. Meanwhile, Dave and I were back in our room hooking a microphone into his prized stereo system.

"Blow my woofers and I'll fuckin' kill you!" he threatened.

"Blow my woofer and I'll follow you anywhere," I replied. God, I'm funny. Finally, we got the whole schmear rigged up and I started practicing scary noises and the like. The noise boomed down the hallway, bouncing off the white brick walls, and for the most part, sounded pretty decent.

But then the coup de grace. It was Crazy Al screaming "turn that shit down Cox and get out here!" Dave and I walked out into the hallway along with Andy and Chris, our two stoner neighbors in 112. Crazy Al was walking down the hallway with something the size of a pumpkin in his hand inside a pillowcase. Everyone gathered around to see what the hell all the ruckus was about.

"Is this your great idea, Al?" I asked.

"Yeah, this is it. This will scare the livin' shit out of those little bastards. Boys … I give you … MR. ED!" With that, Al flung off the pillowcase to reveal the dreaded October surprise.

"Oh shit, what is that?" Feldman grimaced.

"It's a cow's head," said Al. "It's a fuckin' cow's head without the skin on it!!"

"That's fucking disgusting," said Chris.

"Yeah, ain't it? The little shits will take one look at this and piss in their pants."

"I think I already did," I said turning away. The cow's skin had been ripped off to expose bright pink membrane. Al had left its brown eyes in place so you could tell what it was. It also stunk to high heaven.

"Jesus, Al, where'd you get it?" Feldman asked.

"At the farm. We butchered it this morning. This is so great!" He held up Mr. Ed right next to his face and in a shaky voice said, "Wilbur-r-r-r."

◆   ◆   ◆

The kids were due to start arriving at anytime, and we were prepared. The mattresses were on the floor, everyone was armed with a pillow, and our sound system was booming. Mr. Ed had made his home on top of an upside-down trashcan—a blue light focused on his pink face giving it an even more ghoulish look, if that was possible. It was suggested that someone grab somebody from another wing and run them through our haunted wing to see if it was scary or just plain stupid. Dave came back with a girl named Maridy, an anorexic bleached blonde from First West. We turned off all the lights in the hallway and got set up. Dave showed Maridy where to enter.

"WELCOME TO OUR HOUSE!" I announced in my best Dracula impersonation.

At that cue, about ten guys started blindly swinging pillows, hitting each other half the time, and Maridy the other half. She went down like a twenty-dollar whore and crawled the rest of the way cussing the "freaks" out as she went.

"CONTINUE DOWN OUR HALLWAY, IF YOU DARE …"

Maridy walked slowly, the blue light turning her bleached blonde hair a sickly shade of aqua.

"… AND TALK TO MR. ED!!"

Maridy took one look at Mr. Ed, screamed and passed out.

Crazy Al was laughing his ass off. For that matter, so was everyone else. Except Maridy. Word spread quickly that Maridy had bought the farm sort of, and it wasn't long before a ton of people descended down First East to look at Mr. Ed. Between shouts of "gross" and "disgusting" was Big John, with one eye looking at us, and one eye on Mr. Ed. He was not a happy camper.

"This is unacceptable. I hope you guys are happy with what's happened."

We all looked at each other for a moment, and then nodded in agreement. "Yeah, we're pretty happy."

"You guys are assholes!!" Maridy screamed after coming to.

She may have been squeamish, but she was a brilliant judge of character.

7

"Nudity is in the Eye of the Beholder"

—Fathead

An easy way to tell a local Chicoan from a non-resident is the way they pronounce the word "almond." The guy from L.A., take for instance … me, would pronounce it "all-mond." However, a born and raised Chico-type person would say it "a-mon." Their rationale for this silliness is that the fish is called a "sa-mon", not a "sall-mon." You with me so far? There's a joke that revolves around all this bull that Chico almond (choose your favorite pronunciation) growers love to tell. I only hope I can do it justice:

"Seems there was this fella from the city who came and asked me one day, "Is it "all-mond" or "a-mon?" Well, I looked him straight in the eye and said, "Friend, when they're on the trees they're "all-monds" but when it's harvest time, the little boogers don't always like to drop, so we got to shake the "ell" out of the tree. Then they're "a-mons." Get it?"

Gosh, did my ribs ache after hearing that the first time.

◆   ◆   ◆

It was just a couple days after Halloween. The sky was a clear blue, there was the gentle valley breeze stirring through the trees, and the sun warmed to a pleasant 70 degrees. It was too perfect. I was in my room getting changed to go play some volleyball out on the front lawn with a bunch of other dorm mates. So there I was, sitting on my bed, tying my shoes when I looked out the window and saw a set of eyes walk by. The biggest, brownest, most soulful eyes I had ever seen. I rushed out into the lobby with one shoe on my foot and the other in my hand, but I was too late to catch anything more than just a glimpse of a tremendously fine backside walking up the stairs. I turned to the gal behind the desk and inquired as to the name of the love of my life, but she just shrugged and went back to reading her magazine.

I resigned myself to the fact that was going to be the end of my sexual excitement for the day, so I put on my other shoe and went out to play some ball. All through the game, I couldn't get this girl out of my head. Her brown hair, parted on the side, curly but not kinky, draped just at shoulder length. But it was those eyes, those *incredible* eyes, which made me convince myself that I had to meet her. I didn't know her name or anything about her. I just knew I was in love, and my volleyball game was suffering because of it.

A couple of days later I was back out again playing ball. It was a Saturday and it was still sunny and nice so there were people everywhere throwing the Fris or just catching rays. I was playing in the back row, facing Lassen Hall, when I saw her coming. She was riding this beat up old bike down the walkway and as she passed, our eyes met. I continued to stare, oblivious to the game, to the weather and to the outside world. Her hair fell over her left eye in an incredibly sexy fashion, she smiled, and that was that. Like a ghost, her bike was parked and she disappeared inside Shasta. I had asked around on Third West, which was an all girls wing, but no one knew her, so I figured she was on her way to see her boyfriend. Probably some guy named Cliff or Bret. It's all part of what I refer to as: "Mitch's Mystery Boyfriend Theory." In a nutshell, the theory states that:

"If there exists a female that you're interested in, and if that female is not interested in you, and if you ask said female out, and if she says, "No, I have a boyfriend," than that boyfriend's name will be Cliff, Bret, Chuck, Rick or Kyle and not Herman, Myron, Fred, Harold or Irving."

The theory goes on to say that this boyfriend's fat ass will never be seen by you, but since you can't prove he doesn't exist, you're hosed.

Not a half hour went by before this beautiful woman was on her bike riding away from me, her cute little ass moving back and forth as she stood and pedaled. I stared. Then all hell broke loose. She looked back at me and smiled, then just as quickly, disappeared around the bend. I had never believed in love at first sight, but all of a sudden, I understood what it was all about. My heart was somewhere up in my esophagus, and my stomach felt like they were holding a butterfly convention inside.

"Cox, you gonna play ball or what?"

Oh yeah. Volleyball. How could anyone think about volleyball at this point?

◆   ◆   ◆

August 16, 1977 was the day Elvis died. Since then, nonbelievers have espoused theories ranging from the King taking a pressure-relief hiatus in the Caribbean, to hanging around a Burger King in Kalamazoo, Michigan. Now I was a big fan of Elvis, but let's face facts … the guy was a big, fat, drugged out pig when he died. Two years after they buried his bloated corpse, the TV networks still wouldn't let the guy rest in peace. They'd have a slew of those terrible movies he cranked out in assembly-line fashion in the 60s, live concert specials and interviews with a bunch of fat people remembering where they were the day the King died. Why some brainiac up in network control thought anyone would care what some peanut grower was thinking when he heard the news was beyond me, but obviously, somebody did because these shows always got astronomical ratings. Elvis anniversary specials, Elvis anniversary death specials, Elvis anniversary anniversary specials. It got to be so that every day was Elvis day.

On this particular day, it was the 40th anniversary of Elvis getting his first tooth or something like that, so of course, that called for yet another showing of "Elvis, Aloha from Hawaii," a concert film that when originally broadcast in 1973, was beamed to some 80 zillion people. I didn't know all of this until I walked into the TV room where the coke machine was, and saw him gyrating to "Big Hunk o' Love" while tossing out sweat-soaked handkerchiefs to the multitudes. As far as the TV room went, though, the multitudes consisted of this one guy plopped in an easy chair eating sunflower seeds. I had seen him around; in fact I believed he lived on my wing. But he was real quiet, so at the time, I couldn't swear by it. All I knew about him was that he was a hell of a ping-pong player, had one of the best looking girls in the dorm interested in him, though he was too stupid to realize it, and appeared to be a pretty nice guy.

I flipped open my Coke and stood watching the King belt his way through another gem.

"You like Elvis?" I asked.

He spit a bunch of shells into a bag. "He's the King," he said.

Right then, I knew I liked this guy. I sat down in the chair next to him and we shot the breeze for the next couple hours. His name was Steve Nicklos, a sophomore with a business major in the works, who had transferred to Chico after a year of junior college because it felt "just like another year of high school." I had heard those words before.

"You live on my wing, don't you," I asked, and after he confirmed that fact, I asked him how come I never saw him in the hallway or at our thrice-a-week boogie-till-you-puke parties.

"Well, I don't drink for one thing, and, I don't know ... my roommate's kind of weird, so I try to stay away from the wing as much as possible." He went on to tell me a little more about his roommate, a supreme asshole named Jim Hall. Those are my words, not his. Steve never uttered an obscenity that day or ever, as far as I know.

"You play a mean game of ping-pong," I said. "Why don't we play tomorrow after breakfast?"

"I got church at eleven, but I'll be back a little after noon."

"OK," I nodded. Let's see now, the guy doesn't drink, or cuss, or go to parties. But he does go to church. It's a wonder we became best friends.

◆   ◆   ◆

After my disastrous academic year at CSUN, I figured it was time to put a little more effort into class work. I liked college for the simple fact that you got to pick a major and concentrate your studies in that direction. What I didn't like were core classes. This is a group of subjects that some bozos determined were mandatory for everyone to know, else wise they become raging, homicidal maniacs. I had taken a few cores at Northridge, and, despite the fact that I was paying to go to school, was forced to take more at Chico. I had burned up three core units at CSUN by taking Sociology 33, otherwise known as "The Sociology of Sexuality." There was a waiting list ten miles long to get into this class and it was no wonder. We spent probably two out of every three class sessions watching what the instructor referred to as "educational films," but what I referred to as "really hot porn." We had films that showed the progression of an erection, women masturbating, men masturbating, whole families standing in showers masturbating, big tits, small tits, dicks the size of your arm, oral sex, anal sex, the list was endless. The screen we watched this all on was really big and I swear to God if one film didn't have this super-tight close up of some gal's beaver with little graphic arrows pointing out all of the inner workings. After informing us that the clit is here and this is there, the gal shoved about three fingers inside her and started to moan and groan. Girls were getting up in class and running out saying "this is disgusting" while the guys stayed, eyes glued to the screen saying "this is disgusting." As for me, I couldn't take notes fast enough.

So there I was at Chico taking what I assume was another "blow it out your ass" core class. The kind where if you just show up half the time, you get a "B", and if you show up half the time and stay awake, it's an "A." This class was ART-009, Basic Figure Drawing. I took it because I always wanted to be able to draw a nose. I could do a whale of an eye, but I could never draw a decent nose. The class was held in Ayres Hall in a huge classroom with high desks and cold metal stools with no padding virtually assuring your ass would be asleep by the time the hour was up. All the desks were arranged in a circle, like we were awaiting an Indian attack or something. So we're all settling in for our first real day of class when a semi-attractive redhead pulls up to the stool next to me and asks, "Is this Art 9?"

I looked over at her quickly, said "yeah," and went back to what I was doing.

"With Steve Wilson?" she asked.

"Sure is," I said with a smile. A couple of seconds later, out of the corner of my eye, I saw movement. It was kind of an odd movement, one you wouldn't expect to see in an academic class. I looked over at the redhead, and damn if she wasn't taking her clothes off. I looked back at my papers, then back at her, and now she had nothing on from the waist up. After picking my jaw up off the floor, I looked back at my papers, then to the gal to the right of me, then back to the redhead who was now in the process of removing her pants. It's amazing how many thoughts can race helter-skelter through your mind at one time. *Is she crazy? About me? About the instructor? She's got nice tits. Do we all have to do this?* All I knew for sure was that I was really going to like this class.

The door finally swung open and in walked our instructor, a Howdy-Doody clone with a goofy grin. "I see most of you have met our model for today," he said. He waddled around the interior of our circle of desks, flipping on four electric heaters that were all pointed towards the center. Enter stage left our model, butt naked, to stand in various poses for us to draw.

"I want you to draw our model here," said Mr. Wilson. "Her name is Becky. Draw her in any style you want. Use your imagination. I'm not expecting much, after all, this is a beginner class. I just want to see where each of you are starting from."

Mr. Wilson continued to walk around the class, his hands clasped together in front of him like he was praying, explaining to us the importance of artistic illumination, how all we see is light and how it was up to the artist to create the dark or some hooey. He talked about great artists of the past; the impressionists, the realists, the expressionists. He talked about interpreting the figure and allowing the feeling to drive our work. I stared at Becky with the nice tits and the strawberry-blonde muff. That was my interpretation.

After a moment or two of reflection, we all got down to work, pencils furiously pumping away at our paper. Or at least the guys in the class were furiously pumping. Their pencils, that is. Most of the women drew either surrealistic images of some sort, or concentrated on Becky's upper body, say ... above the shoulders. The guys, on the other hand, drew tits. And muff. And tits and muff. And all the tits they drew were much larger than Becky's original factory equipment.

After about ten or fifteen minutes, Becky would change poses and we would all sketch again. On the fourth or fifth pose, she sat her butt down on a little piece of carpet in the center of the circle and crossed her legs in the yoga style position. This exposed a part of her usually reserved for magazines with foldouts. The gal next to me muttered how she had "just about enough of this" grabbed her sketchbook and walked out. Everyone in the room thought the same thing about her at that point. She was a tight-ass prude who wouldn't be back to ART 009 ever again.

But she did come back the next Tuesday. And so did Becky, and me, and Howdy-Doody, and the rest of the class. After the initial shock of this woman stripping to her birthday suit had worn off, we all got used to the whole procedure and started to try serious artwork.

Then one session, Becky didn't show up for class. Howdy-Doody walked in with this guy who looked like he just stepped out of Muscle & Fitness magazine. He had curly brown hair, deep set eyes, a chiseled chin and all he was wearing was a yellow tank top and black silk running shorts. His arms had muscles on top of their muscles, and his legs looked like bridge supports. God, apparently, was enrolling in our ART 009 class.

"All right, guys," Howdy-Doody announced, "this is Mike. He's going to be our model for today."

"Right on!" the one-time, tight-ass prude next to me said.

Our buddy Mike then ripped of his shirt and dropped his shorts. In case you weren't aware of this, God is hung like a Hebrew National.

"Right on!" she said again.

We all got to work while muscle-bound Mike posed in various statuesque poses. Looking at a guy standing there with his Johnson hanging out reminded me just how truly ugly the human body is in comparison to other animals. You throw a horse or a puppy or something else up against the human form and it's no contest. Other animals have a full coat of fur, while humans look like they just got out of chemotherapy. Even this guy, for all his chiseled good looks and brick shithouse body, looked really stupid up there.

I, along with I assume the rest of the guys in class, took great pains to draw Mike's face. Some even went as far as the chest. The slut next to me, the same one who had stormed off when Becky was tastefully posing, was now drawing penises the size of your arm.

"You're so shallow," I said to her.

"Right on."

"You know, there's more to the male species than … that!" I said, pointing an accusing finger at the vile smut she had drawn.

"What about you?" she replied, "As I recall, you didn't complain too much when that girl was up there."

"That's different," I confidently said. "That was art."

She shook her head, not swayed by my obviously superior debate skills.

"Men," she muttered.

"Slut," I said.

8

○ ○

"The only thing we have to fear, is beer itself"

—*Franklin Delano "Fathead" Roosevelt*

I drank my first beer my second month at Chico. I had tasted beer before, when our family would go out to a Mexican restaurant and Dad would offer Kerry and me a sip of his Dos Equis. But I'm talking my very own first full bottle of beer. I was nineteen years old.

Dave and Chris were having a party next door in 112, so I went over and joined the fracas. It took me a millennium to empty my first Michelob, but I did it and at least in the field of alcoholism, I was no longer a virgin. Funny thing about beer, you ask ten people if they like the taste and nine of them will respond negatively. They'll tell you it's a taste you have to "acquire."

"Why I should I acquire a taste for something that tastes like dog piss?" I asked.

"Because you can't get fucked up on dog piss," Crazy Al replied.

The fact that I had now consumed my first beer failed to impress the Freaks. They just handed me another and told me to try and finish this one before graduation.

Another hour or so later, the deed had been accomplished. Two beers. Down. History. Dust. Twenty-four ounces of hops and grains and pure Rocky Mountain spring water. Boy, was I drunk.

"Cox, you're a lightweight!" some asshole said.

"Fuck you." Alcohol was great for my wit.

At this point, someone suggested we hit the midnight movie at the El Rey Theater. Midnight movies are especially popular in college towns for a variety of reasons, most of which have nothing to do with cinematic entertainment. That night, the big feature was the cult classic, *The Rocky Horror Picture Show*. We all went and shelled out our two bucks, grabbed a whole row of seats in the balcony and started to yell and scream like baboons. I was feeling great while we were

39

walking over to the El Rey in the cool fall air. I was feeling okay when we all sat down to wait for the movie to begin. But once the lights went low, and the screen lit up, it was time for the fat lady to start singing because this opera was over.

I can't remember anything specific about the movie because I had apparently killed every one of my brain cells with two lousy beers. I recall vaguely all these freaky people singing and running around, but I didn't have a clue as to why. The movie was not making me feel very well. In fact, I was getting real sleepy, so I closed my eyes.

BIG MISTAKE #1

Those little green squares I normally see when I close my eyes were now doing the beer barrel polka inside my head. They just kept going round and round and round. So, I opened my eyes.

BIG MISTAKE #2

There was more singing and running around and fat people and weird people and shit falling from the roof and yelling. This was the worst movie in the world. So I closed my eyes again.

THIRD AND FINAL BIG MISTAKE

Tropical storm Michelob hit my brain with gale force winds. Those little green squares, the ones that used to be so organized, now blew helter-skelter in different directions across my mental landscape. My head rotated around clock-wise like a gyroscope trying in a vain attempt to catch up. Then, someone punched me in the stomach, or at least it felt like it. I stood up, fell on top of Feldman, picked myself up and went stumbling down the stairs, through the lobby, out the door, down Second Street, past the Madison Bear Garden, to the grass in front of Laxson Auditorium where I promptly proceeded to puke my guts out.

All of a sudden, I was as tired as I could ever remember being. I somehow made it across campus to Shasta. Fortunately, Dave had left the room unlocked; because there was no way in hell I would have been able to stick the key in the lock. I collapsed on the bed wondering why anyone in their right mind would do this to themselves on purpose, and then to top it off, refer to it as "fun."

"I'm never going to drink again," I said before passing out.

All of this on account of two beers.

◆   ◆   ◆

It was now the beginning of our third month at Chico in general, and Shasta in particular. Not only had three hundred-plus strangers become acquaintances if not friends, some were becoming more than friends. Dave had started going out with this great gal named Kim Schuloff. She was one of those kinds of people that could energize a room just by walking in. It helped that she was quite attractive and had a great body, but even if she hadn't, her personality would have been enough.

One of the problems of living in the dorms was a complete lack of privacy. Dave and I shared one small room with no walls or doors or anything to divide us. His bed was no more than six feet away from mine. We had devised a signal at the beginning of their relationship to let me know if I could or could not enter the room. I had taken an old record album and played Frisbee in the hallway with it till it busted in half. I then tacked one half to the door and created a super-secret code that only Dave, myself and pretty much the rest of the dorm knew. If the round part of the record was down, all was cool and I could go on in. If, however, the round part was on top, then I should go away and come back later. This system worked flawlessly for about three days, until the day I went to the room to pick up some books for class and the record was in the "go away" position. I stood outside the room debating with myself whether I should go in or just go to class without my books. The debate was over quickly. I had to have those books, and what the hell, I thought, it was my room as much as his.

I pulled out my keys and started jingling them loud enough for the whole dorm to hear.

"Just need to get a few books and get back to class," I yelled over the rinky-tink sound of my keys jangling together.

I paused for a moment. Silence. Then I heard Kim's distinctive Huckleberry Hound laugh, kind of "yuk, yuk, yuk" and then, "come on in, Mitchums!" invitation. And that's how it went from then on. The busted record was removed from the door permanently, and the new rules of "key jingling before entering" were enforced.

After a while, Dave, Kim and I were like roommates. I had become used to changing in front of Dave, but not in front of Kim. So when the time came to go to bed, and Kim and Dave were there, I would politely ask her to turn her head. This too came to pass as I got tired of asking her to subsidize my modesty and just dropped my pants whenever it was appropriate.

Then the lights would be shut off and the fireworks would begin. There would be talking amongst the three of us for a few minutes before one of us offered the first "goodnight."

"Goodnight, Mitchums!" Kim would say. I've never been called "Mitchums" by any other person in my life prior or since.

"Night Kim ... night Dave."

"Later."

And then the only sound was the muffled shouts of the Freaks down the hall, or a door slamming or the low hum of the heater. For five, maybe ten minutes, my eyes would close and I would attempt to fall asleep. Then, the whispering would begin, barely audible to the human ear, but loud and penetrating enough to prevent me from the almighty snooze. There would be a rustling of sheets. It was like an old Western where the sheriff says, "it's awful quiet out there ... a little too quiet," seconds before his soldiers got their brains blown out by a jillion Indians. Those guys were always waiting for the inevitable snap of a dry twig. I, on the other hand, was waiting for the inevitable squeak of the bed spring. Dave and Kim would continue whispering, but I could only imagine what they were saying—probably tender words of love, or something close to it. Then it would happen. Dave's cot springs would creak with delight. Just once; then twice; then three times. Then bring out the orchestra and let's take it home. As Dave went in-and-out, the springs went up-and-down and in between the grunting and groaning and squeaking and creaking, I'd be wide awake, pretending to be asleep. For some reason, I would barely open one eye to try and watch them for fear they might see me and get mad—as if they had nothing else on their minds at the time.

Sex, sex, sex. God, did they have sex. At the time, it was the closest I had ever come to sleeping with a woman. In retrospect, it must have been just as difficult for them to experience the incredible joys of lovemaking with some buck-toothed virgin listening in a body length away. Eventually, the festivities would end culminating with Dave letting out a loud grunt similar to that of the African hippo. The squeaking would stop, the whispering would begin anew, and I would lie there for hours wondering what it must be like to be actually inside a woman. Then, after a while, I'd finally crash for good and dream about someone who I didn't know and never would. In the morning, I'd wake up and Kim would be gone, and Dave would sit on the edge of his bed, yawning and scratching himself, his eyes drooping like a bloodhound. Then he'd look down at himself and say, "nothing like an early morning hard-on."

What a stud.

9

"I'm going to join the club and beat you over the head with it."

—*Groucho "Fathead" Marx*

As far as I know, I never met anyone who truly hated me. I've had people who didn't like me, dare I say, maybe even became nauseous at the very sight of me, but never one who thoroughly and unequivocally loathed me.

Except for Jim Hall.

Jim was Steve's roommate at the end of First East. When the "Freaks" first started getting together for parties and such, he seemed like one of the guys. A little uglier than most, with his Fu Manchu moustache and razor thin eyes, but one of the guys just the same. He came from a town called Hollister whose only claim to fame is that they supposedly have at least one earthquake there every day of the year. I guess the town is located directly on the San Andreas Fault or something, and the residents there have gotten used to a mild tremor on a daily basis. From what I could figure, Jim had his brains shook up one too many times. Jim, as they say, was not wired for cable.

So one day I was walking down the hallway toward cellblock #110 and I saw Jim at the very far end of the wing unlocking the door to his room.

"Hey, Cox …," he yelled.

He had always called me Mitch before, but I figured what the heck, I'd play along. "Hey, Hall!" I yelled back.

"Yeah? Well fuck you, you son-of-a-bitch asshole!"

"What?" I said, clearly hearing him, but not quite understanding what this was all about.

"You heard me you pussy fuck asshole dickhead!" he screamed as he dropped whatever it was he was carrying and headed down the hall for me. Jim always walked like he was headed for the big shootout with Wild Bill Hickok or something. He swaggered on down the hall towards me, babbling obscenities in no particular order. I decided that while I thought Jim was truly an idiot, it would be more idiotic of me to wait for him so that he could beat the crap out of me or whatever he had in mind, so I jumped inside my room and locked it tight behind me.

And waited.

But nothing happened. Jim didn't come down and pound on the door, or threaten to "huff and puff and blooowwww my house down" so I blew it off to his assholiness being drunk or something. I did keep the door locked and chained however, just to be on the safe side.

So the next day, virtually the same circumstances occurred. I had just come back from some boring class and all I wanted to do is change into some sweats and maybe play a little ping-pong, but there was Jim at the end of the hall and damn it if he didn't once again let loose with a torrent of nonsensical four-letter words.

"Cox, you motherfucker, I ought to kick your ass, cocksucker," he bellowed.

"Jim, what is your problem?" I said, trying to reason with the baboon. "Did I do something to piss you off?"

"Fuck you, asshole!'

Oh.

At that point, I gathered it was useless to try and negotiate with someone with the intelligence of a bar of soap, so I started egging him on.

Not surprisingly, this seemed to piss him off more, and once again, he started heading down the hallway ready to do battle. And once again, I opened my door and jumped inside the safety of my little home away from home. Now this is not to say that I'm a chicken. I just don't believe in fighting unless I absolutely have to. Mainly because I have a tendency to get the snot beat out of me. My best friend growing up, coincidentally also named Jim, used to hit me in the stomach about a zillion times just to keep me in line, whereupon, I would run home to my brother who would then beat the holy hell out of Jim. Jim, in turn, would run to his brother Rick who would clobber my brother, who would then beat me up because he didn't have an older brother he could ask to beat Rick up. It wouldn't have mattered anyway, because Jim and Rick had an older brother Bob, and we had plumb run out of brothers.

Anyway, this crap continued for another few weeks, and at one time, we almost came to blows, but fortunately for me, there were a couple guys around to break it up before it got ugly. Ugly as in me getting the living crap beat out of me. The story does have a happy ending, however. Jim finally got tired of threatening me and started in on the guy that lived across the hall from him. This dude's name was Scott, and he was just as stupid as Jim. Scott's big thing was to walk up to me and say, "Hey Mitch, guess how tall I am."

Now Scott was not a giant or anything, but I guess he thought he was, so I used to play along. "Gosh Scott, I don't know, maybe ... five-foot, eleven?"

"I'm six-three!"

At this point, I would expound countless adjectives of admiration for his hugeness. We did this routine at least once a week for God knows what reason.

But anyway, Jim started threatening Scott, calling him a "blind motherfucker" because Scott was about half-blind and getting worse. Then one day, Jim pulled a rifle out of his closet and pointed it at Scott and thus ended the brief, but illustrious college career of Jim Hall. The Chico Police came down and dragged his sorry ass out in handcuffs, and all the while that Jim was kicking and screaming and cussing, we were waving a fond farewell and sharing a good laugh.

◆   ◆   ◆

It only took me a couple of months to really fall in love with Chico. Since I couldn't get a girl, I might as well get intimate with a town.

Downtown Chico, the side nearest the school and the oldest part of town, is about nine blocks long lined with buildings that have been there in one form or another since the 1800s. Most have been remodeled into hip clothing stores, or music stores or whatever college people are into at the time. There were plenty of bars from the traditional Town Lounge that everyone referred to as the "Scrounge Lounge" because of their high-end clientele, to a wild place called the Madison Bear Garden. This was considered the place to go if you went to Chico, lived in Chico, or were just visiting Chico. It wasn't fancy at all, in fact, it looked like someone had built a real beautiful museum, only to have the whole thing get the shit blown out of it by a tornado. There was stuff everywhere; on the ceiling, coming out of the walls, everywhere. Moose heads, bicycles, mannequins of naked women, anything you could think of was glued to the ceiling ready to fall into your Bear Burger. Upstairs was the smallest dance floor in the world, but this was not the place to go dance. This was the place to go to with friends, pick up women and get ripped. College life was so educational.

About a mile outside of the downtown area was the beginning of Bidwell Park, one of the largest municipal parks in the country. The name "Bidwell" is synonymous with "mom," "apple pie," and "God" up in that area for the simple fact that if it wasn't for John and Annie Bidwell, there would be no park, no University and hence, no town worth a pitcher of warm spit, to quote John Nance

Garner. John and Annie settled up in the North Valley before the turn of the century when there wasn't much up there besides rice fields and a zillion Chinese. They purchased the land that now encompasses all of the University and the park running west to east about ten miles following Big Chico Creek up into the foothills. Their house, which still stands today and is classified as a historical landmark, was built in the standard Victorian design of the period with windows coming out of every which-way and nooks on top of their crannies. But it was home so they painted it Annie's favorite color. Pink. Bright pink. God-awful, ugly pink. And when I say pink, I don't just mean pink, I mean stand on top of Butte Hall with a megaphone screaming "PINK!" These two may have been the cat's pajamas when it came to real estate, but one could only have wished that they'd let someone else do the interior decorating.

So around 1888 or thereabouts, John and Annie decided to do something for the community and thus the beginning of my dear alma mater. The students, all women, lived upstairs in the mansion with John and Annie downstairs making sure that none of them smoked, drank or cussed. This was not a party-down, gaggle of gals at this point, and it's hard to believe that the school the teetotaling Bidwells founded would be named the number one party school in the nation one hundred years later.

My knowledge of what happened after that is minimal. Let's just say that the school grew larger and larger and was transformed into Chico State Teachers College. John and Annie bought the farm, surrealistically speaking, and in their will left about 600 acres for the expansion of the school and the rest of the land to the town with the stipulation that it be turned into a park. Also, in the will, though no one *ever* abides by it, is a small part that says that there is to be no alcohol of any sort on their property. Oh well, two out of three ain't bad.

Exactly one mile from downtown heading into the park is a big swimming and recreational area cleverly named One Mile for the previously stated reason. Besides the usual assortment of horseshoe pits, ball fields and chirping squirrels that all parks are required by law to have, One Mile also boasted one of the largest swimming holes in the state. Actually, it isn't really a pool, but more of a lake. The city dams up Big Chico Creek letting just a bit of water through thus not only creating the swimming area, but Little Chico Creek in the process.

A tree-lined bike trail leaving One Mile winds its way through the park in route to the next recreation area four miles away. Once again, Chico's civic leaders put their collective heads together and came up with an exciting, yet descriptive name. I'll give you a hint: it's five miles from downtown.

At Five Mile Recreation Area, there were once again horseshoe pits, softball fields, chirping squirrels, and something that wasn't at One Mile; a huge monstrosity by the name of Hooker Oak. Yet another in the long line of historical monument-type attractions this town boasts, was this enormous oak tree that was somewhere in the neighborhood of 500 million years old. Its branches were as thick as most trees trunks, and they spread out in a spastic manner covering an area the size of Nebraska. A few years after I arrived in town, one of ol' Hooker's branches fell off and clunked some lady on the head killing her faster than you can say "Paul Bunyun." This initiated a flurry of lawsuits by her kin against the town, the county, the state, the squirrels that lived in the damn tree, and anybody or anything that had even the remotest connection to maintaining the safety of park goers. It was settled out of court with the plaintiffs getting a bucket load of money, and poor old Hooker getting the chainsaw. All that's left of this magnificent tree, this living historical document, is a stump and a sign that says something like:

<u>HOOKER OAK</u>

The largest oak tree in the continental United States, Hooker Oak was over 60 feet high and 100 feet wide. Its trunk was the size of a small pickup, and it was once the home for the entire Swiss Air Force. It's really too bad that a branch fell off onto a lady's head causing the state to turn this beautiful, historical landmark into 10,000 bundles of kindling.

Or something like that …

10

o o o o o o o o o o o o o o o o o o o o o o o o o o o o o o o o

"The Russians are coming, the Russians are coming, and they're really pissed."

—*Boris "Fathead" Yeltsin*

After my pathetic academic performance at Cal State Northridge, I was determined to improve the all important grade point average at Chico. I had graduated high school with a cumulative 3.33 GPA, not exactly Ivy League material, but an average that most students would have been happy to have. I still didn't study very hard, but I knew that as winter finals approached, I couldn't simply get away with bullshitting my professors. I had to give it my best shot, and that meant devoting time every night to the books.

I was confident that I would do well in all my classes except for Art. Ever since that redhead had stopped taking her clothes off in class, Art had become a tedious rundown of muscle location and bone identification. I kind of understood what this had to do with the ability to properly draw the human figure, but it seemed to have gone a bit overboard. Howdy-Doody informed us that our final would consist of identifying and locating every muscle and bone in the human body. No drawing, no sketching, no naked women.

Dave the roomie was still going out with Kim, who just happened to be a nursing student, so I figured that if I was close enough friends to undress in front of her, I could certainly study with her. And God, did we study. Every night, Kim and I, and a few of her nursing student friends, would hibernate in the study hall at Shasta pouring over notes and such trying desperately to make sense of the human body. They quizzed me on metacarpals, metatarsals, gastrointestinal muscles and the like.

"Where is the tibia?" she asked.

"I don't know, somewhere near Egypt I think."

"What is the latissimus dorsi?"

"It's a kind of fish."

"Name the three sections of vertebrae."

"Larry, Moe and Curly."

And so it went. I felt like a Goddamn med student. I just wanted to learn how to draw a nose.

Finally, D-Day had nearly arrived. It was a Sunday night in December. Christmas break was in the back of everyone's mind, but it needed to stay there for now, for tomorrow was the first day of finals. My first final was scheduled for Monday morning at 10. It was Art 9. I studied all day, breaking just long enough to grab some lunch at Whitney where my daily choice consisted of a hot dog or a sandwich made with the universally feared "green loaf imitation meat-by-product." I chose the hot dog.

Anyway, I was going to know this shit inside and out. By Sunday evening, I started feeling a bit strange, like someone had drawn the shades on my brain. I sat with Kim in the study going over everything we had already gone over one hundred times previously.

"Are you okay?" she asked.

"I don't know. I feel like my head weighs about a thousand pounds."

"Maybe we should just call it a night," she said, closing the books.

"I just feel so damn tired. My stomach feels rotten … everything. Maybe it was the Whitney dog." I was in first class whiner mode.

Kim put her hand on my head to feel for a temperature. After peeling what remained of her fingers off my forehead, she walked me down to my room telling me her roommate was feeling the same way. "In fact, there's a bunch of people upstairs who are sick. I think something's going around."

"Great timing," I said, falling face first into bed.

The next morning the alarm went off. At least I guess it did because I sure never heard it. Dave was trying to wake me up, but at that point, the London Philharmonic couldn't have got me out of bed. My whole body felt like lead. Lead wearing cement underwear in a big vat of Jell-O. I was able to crawl over to the phone and call Mr. Wilson's office.

"Oh God, please be there, please be there … answer the damn … oh, Mr. Wilson? This is Mitch Cox from your Art 9 Tuesday-Thursday … yeah, that's why I'm calling … I feel like shit, I mean really horrible … yeah … yeah … well, I didn't know that I was going to be sick … just let me take it in a couple of days … no … yeah … yeah … that wouldn't be fair to the other students but … swell … bye."

Short and sweet. Mr. Wilson bluntly informed me that if I wanted to delay my final, I had to have submitted a written request on a form 39-A three weeks in advance to both him and the department head. Needless to say, I hadn't done that. I tried in vain to tell him that three weeks ago, I didn't know that my body would presently feel like it had been run over by a big-rig. He was to say the least, unsympathetic; to say the most, an asshole.

How I got to school, found my way to class, remembered my number-two pencil, and took the test is still one of life's great unsolved mysteries. I do remember Mr. Wilson shaking me a few times during the test in a feeble attempt to keep me awake. It would last for about five minutes or so before my forehead would hit the tabletop with a resounding thud.

"Mr. Cox, you need to take this test, and to do so, you need to stay awake," he politely whispered in my ear.

"I mumbled something about being "so tired" and "so weak" but I kept wishing inside that I would find the strength to throw up on his shoes. After about an hour and a half of this futility, I grabbed my test and trudged up to where this Howdy-Doody son-of-a-bitch teacher of mine was sitting.

"How'd we do?" he asked casually.

"We would have done a lot better if you'd had let me take the test when I didn't feel so shitty."

"I'm sure you'll do fine."

It's at this point where it is customary to tell the teacher how much you enjoyed taking his class, and how you sincerely wish to have him relating his vast wealth of knowledge to you again in the near future.

"Eat me," I said.

So I was close.

I went back to my room immediately after another in the continuing saga of "Mitch Goes to the Can" and collapsed. I woke up a few hours later and made my way to the college infirmary, where, after several blood tests and other assorted poking and prodding, it was determined that I, along with a good many others at Shasta, had been infected with the H1N1 virus, also known as "The Russian Flu." If this, I thought, is how all Russians feel, it's no wonder they've got a gigantic piece of crap for a country.

After swallowing gobs of pills, and sleeping the rest of the day and night away, I was feeling as fit as a slightly out-of-tune fiddle. And, despite the fact that I could barely stay awake through the entire ugly process, I managed to get a "C" on the Art final. To me, that proved that I knew the stuff like the back of my metacarpals … or is it metatarsals?

11

o o o o o o o o o o o o o o o o o o o o o o o o o o o o o o o o o o o
"I will study no more, forever."

—Chief "Fathead" Joseph

Finals week.

Like I said, I was determined that I was going to get off on the right foot at Chico and not try to sleaze my way through my classes like I did at Northridge. I had taken copious notes in class, completed all the assignments in a timely manner, and asked the professors insightful and probing questions.

I even went to the library.

At Northridge, I would go to the library between classes and spend my time reading old National Lampoon magazines and laughing my ass off. At Chico, the library for some unexplained reason didn't carry old copies of the National Lampoon. So I'd walk around for awhile, looking for someone to talk to. I'd see a few people I'd recognize, but they were always buried six feet into their books and weren't interested in shooting the breeze. Eventually, I'd give up the search, settle back in one of those soft cushioned chairs, the kind where you need a Tommy-Lift to extricate yourself, and begin to study whatever it was I was supposed to study. Boy, was that boring. At that point, I developed a theory about studying that I relied on all through the rest of my time at Chico.

Cox's Theory of Studying:

Read all of your notes (this theory does require superior note taking skills) three times the night before your test. Then, right as you're sitting at your desk getting ready to take the test, read all your notes again skipping nothing. The last glance will trigger oodles of memory cells into action and the test will be a piece of cake.

I tried pushing this idea on some of the guys on the wing, but they wouldn't buy it. Larry, for instance, seemed to spend every waking hour in the library or in Shasta's study hall immersed in engineering books. I never saw anyone study so much, for so long, for so little.

51

"Larry," one of us would whisper, poking our head into the study. "We're havin' a party in Chris and Dave's room, why don't you come down?"

You could tell he really wanted to, but that crazy thing called guilt would remind him he needed to study.

"Naahh, I can't."

"C'mon!"

"Maybe later," he'd say just to get us to leave him alone. I always liked Larry. He was just a real nice guy; tall, blonde, looked like he had just walked off the beach at Malibu. So I tried to let him in on *Cox's Theory of Studying.*

"It doesn't work like that, Mitch. You got to do all this other stuff here," he said pointing to reams of graph paper, slide rules and other engineering-type paraphernalia.

"Larry, look at it this way," I said, trying to be logical. "You could study every day, every night, till your eyes bleed. Study, study, study. And then you could go take your test and still bomb. With my method, you spend a lot less time studying."

"But you could still bomb."

"Of course you could, but you have a lot more time to have fun instead of studying, and you *could* get an "A". To me, it would kill me to spend all that time, time that I could be doing something I enjoy, studying, and then go in and shit the bed. This way, I may bomb the test, but I wouldn't be so mad at myself for wasting so much time on it."

"But I need to study more than just looking at my notes a couple of times," he said.

"First off, it's not just 'looking at your notes a couple of times.' It's carefully studying them word for word three times. It's like mentally re-writing your notes each time. In fact, an even more effective way is to actually, physically, re-write your notes three times. I'm doing that for my Psych final. I swear to God, Larry, it works for me."

That last line was key. It did work for me. Larry went back to pouring over his books and journals and what not, and I walked out of the study knowing that I had learned something about myself. My theory of studying worked for me, for the simple fact that, despite my D+ at Northridge, school was never really very hard for me. I had always known that I was of at least above average intelligence, but now I understood what that meant. It meant that I could get away with *Cox's Theory of Studying* while someone like Larry couldn't. He had to do it his way, the way that felt best for him. I sat down in the lobby and thought about that for a long time. The next day, I would ace my Psych final and Larry would flunk his engineering exam and be put on academic probation. I wished I could have taken back everything I said to him that night.

12

"Give me liberty, or give me death. Or at least introduce me to
your sister."

—Nathan "Fathead" Hale

Obsession. To be obsessed. Joe was obsessing. No … that's not right. Never did
quite figure out if it was a verb or an adjective or both, and damn if I was going to
look it up.

My obsession was the woman in black—the one with the enormous brown
eyes. The sexiest, most beautiful woman I had ever seen. Ever since I saw her walk
into Shasta that one day, I was completely and forever hers. Only problem was
that little episode happened nearly six months previous and I had yet to find out
her name, much less anything else about her. But still, I saw her a couple times a
week, catching a glimpse of her as she walked down the pathway towards the
dorms, then rushing out into the lobby to try and catch her eye. She probably
thought my ass had been glued to the easy chair in the lobby, but I didn't care.

Then one spring day, I was just shootin' the breeze with this guy I had nick-
named "Coach." I called him that because he always wore his keys around his
neck on a string and for some reason, I always thought there was a whistle there
too. Anyway, there I am talking to Coach when I turned around and came face to
face with my obsession. She kind of tilted her head down and to the side so that
her hair fell down over her left eye. The she said, very softly, like a feather landing
on a cloud, "Hi."

I just about came in my pants.

Fortunately, however, I managed instead to spit out a "Hi" out of blind
instinct and then, like a flash, she was gone, up the stairs and out of earshot of my
panting.

"Do you know who she is, what her name is, anything?" I breathlessly asked
Coach.

He shrugged and shook his head. "She goes and sees one of the guys on Second East like almost every day."

"Who?"

"I don't know."

I was incredulous. "What do you mean you don't know?! You live on the Goddamn floor!"

"I'm on Second West," Coach protested.

What a jerk, I thought. If this mystery woman ever came down my wing, I'd know the names, ages and birthdates of all her Goddamn cousins for Chrissakes. "Can you find out for me who she goes to see?"

"Yeah, I guess," he replied rather unenthusiastically.

After letting him know what a grand example of humankind I thought he was, I started fantasizing about my chances with the girl. Walks hand in hand, romantic dinners with candlelight and wine even though I couldn't stand the stuff because it always made my ears itch, slow dancing in each others arms till late in the evening. Then home for a night of passionate lovemaking.

Meanwhile, Dave and Kim were doing the big nasty a lot. I mean a lot. I wasn't getting any sleep whatsoever lying there with one eye open watching Dave's silhouette going up and down, praying that afterwards, Kim would dance around naked and come shake her tits in my face. That never happened. But that never kept me from hoping it would. Trying to sleep out in the study was equally useless for if it wasn't the endless, "What the hell you doin' out here, Cox?" questions, it was the deafening silence of people studying and the horrifying thought that I might fart loudly after falling asleep.

After throwing my books on the desk one day and dropping like a sack of cement onto my bed with an ever so subtle, "Jesus Christ, I'm tired," Dave caught on to the fact that this arrangement was going to be the death of me.

"How's it going with what's-her-name?" he asked.

"Swell," I said disgustedly, face first into my pillow.

There was a long pause.

"What *is* her name?"

"I … don't … know," I said, like I needed to be reminded of this.

Dave got up to leave, but instead, stopped and stood directly over me. I turned over to see his steely-blue eyes looking right through me.

"Mitch, before this year is out, I want you to kick me out of this room for one night."

"Yeah, right."

"I want to sleep in the study," he continued.

"So do it, believe me, there's plenty of room." I was in no mood for this.

"I mean it, Mitch. I want you to kick me out."

"So get out!" I think I was becoming a little sensitive about my continuing virginity.

Dave turned and left, satisfied that he had given me the morale boost I needed. All it did, in reality, was make me even more depressed. What the hell, I thought. I'm never going to know this girl's name much less go to bed with her. Find someone! Anyone! For God sakes, there's got to be some fat pig that's just as desperate to lose her cherry. No, I thought. You got your pride. Wait a minute, what about Linda? Yeah … what about Linda?

Linda Jacobs lived on Third East where all the quiet, studious type lived. She was an interesting girl; a wonderful combination of intelligence, beauty and mystery. I would go up to her room some nights, and we'd sit on her bed and talk about God knows what for hours. Then, at some point in the conversation, she'd stare at me, her green eyes blazing a trail through her brown, kinky hair, and say something to the effect of how sometimes she felt like attacking me.

"I feel the same way about you," I'd cleverly respond.

There'd be this long silence, and inside my brain, this little dude would be screaming at the top of his lungs, "TAKE THE HINT YOU ASSHOLE!" while at the same time, this other little wimpy guy would say, "Don't take a chance. You might get rejected and your poor self-image, psychologically speaking, would get the shit kicked out of it."

For some pathetic reason, I've always tended to follow the advice of the little wimpy guy.

"What should we do about this?" she purred, moving closer to me on the bed. We'd look at each other for what seemed like hours, or at least the length of a Love Boat episode. Our faces would draw closer, her bottom lip quivering with anticipation. God, I wanted that woman.

"TAKE HER YOU ASSHOLE!" little dude #1 would scream.

And I'd move closer, and the wimpy guy would chime in.

"You start with her, and one thing is going to lead to another and you'll want to have sex with her, and then you're going to drop your pants and she's going to laugh her brains out."

Great. Even my subconscious made small penis jokes. Nah, that doesn't matter, I would think. Every magazine article I ever read written by one of those so-called "sex experts" would say that size doesn't matter. So how come every guy in Penthouse describes himself as the possessor of a "nine-inch throbbing missile of love" or having "eight inches of the hardest salami this side of Italy?" Just once, just once, I'd like to read about the guy with the dick "about the size of a chicken frank."

So Linda and I would end up in a staring contest like I used to do with my dog, but unfortunately, in this case, I always blinked first. When Linda couldn't detect any significant movement emanating from my side, she would gracefully end the tension.

"I would attack you Mitch, except of course, for Tucker."

Ah yes, Tucker. Tucker Coolidge, if you can believe that. The mystery boyfriend. This yahoo supposedly lived up near Lake Tahoe somewhere doing who knows what for a living. Linda showed me a picture of him once, I guess to prove to me that he really did exist. To be perfectly honest, with a name like Tucker Coolidge, I expected to see some six-foot-two black guy, not some long-haired reject from Woodstock. He may have existed, but I'll bet his real name was Wally or Stan and not Tucker.

◆   ◆   ◆

Time was running out. It was mid-April and still, no action, still no prospect of any action, and my sexual peak from what I had read, was going to end in a matter of months. I had set a goal for the end of my first year at Chico, and it had nothing to do with grades. I was going to have sex with someone, anyone, before my twentieth birthday or I was going to join a monastery. This was my own, private little secret, but one that I mulled over in my head as I lied out in the spring sun.

"Her name's Janet," a voice said from behind me.

I opened my eyes and was instantly blinded by the noon day sun. "What?"

Coach kneeled down next to me. "Her name's Janet."

I sat up quickly like someone had stuck a cattle prod up my ass. "How'd you find out?"

"Just asked around," he said.

It was time for the key question; the question that would hold the answer to all of life's hopes and dreams.

"Who's she always going to see?" I said, praying it wasn't a boyfriend with a chiseled chin.

"You know Tim Finnell?" he asked, referring to this tall, good looking guy with one long eyebrow that lived on the second floor.

"Yeah, is that her boyfriend?"

"It's her brother."

I sprang up and knocked Coach on his ass as I ran by him. I flung open the glass door to Shasta so hard it almost broke and raced upstairs to Second East. There was a guy coming out of the bathroom with just a towel wrapped around his waist.

"Which room's Tim Finnell in?" I said anxiously. The guy gave me a couple of "umms" and "ahhs" while I danced around like I had to go pee.

"232, end of the hall," he finally said.

I shot past him like a cruise missile and burst into the room to find Tim sitting on the bed harmlessly tying his shoes. Before he could even say "hi" or "what the hell are you doing in my room?" I had him by the lapels, our noses just inches apart.

"INTRODUCE ME TO YOUR SISTER!" I screamed.

◆   ◆   ◆

As I walked downstairs, my heart still beating like a madman, I began to realize what an incredibly stupid thing I had just done. First off, if Janet, the love of my life, the woman of my dreams, etc., etc. had been there, that would have been a fine how-do-you-do. Second, if I was ever going to score with this babe, I had to be tight with her brother because she obviously liked him or she wouldn't be visiting him all the time. I had to assume Tim didn't appreciate the shit being scared out of him, especially by someone who just wanted to get into his little sister's pants, so I tried being real buddy-buddy with him for the next few days. Our conversations would be strictly small talk ending with the familiar refrain, "so, when are you going to introduce me to your sister?"

"Stand in line," he said one day.

"What do you mean?" I asked, looking somewhat like a wounded puppy.

"Ask Darryl and Fats."

"Darryl and Fats? Give me a break!" Darryl was this curly-haired guy who when he would talk to you, would look you up and down like a Goddamn surveyor. Even though we ended up friends for the most part, the guy was an asshole. And Fats was the nickname for one of the Residence Advisors named Kevin. I guess the guy won a couple games of pool once in his life, thus the nickname.

"Darryl's an asshole!" I argued, trying desperately to move up in the rankings.

"Yeah, so is Fats," Tim replied.

"Right, so is Fats!" I agreed.

"And so are you."

He had me there.

"Look Mitch," he continued. "Jan's not your type. Believe me, you two have absolutely nothing in common. You're like on opposite ends of the Earth. You're the North Pole, she's the South Pole. Do you understand what I'm saying? She's not who you think she is. You and her are oil and water. Same with Darryl and Fats. You guys just aren't the kind of guy she goes out with, okay?"

I thought about what Tim had said for a moment. Then I thought of Janet's incredible, soulful brown eyes.

"So, when are you going to introduce me to your sister?"

◆   ◆   ◆

It didn't take long. Just a couple days later, I was on my way to class when I heard Tim say, "Mitch, come over here for a second, there's someone I'd like you to meet."

I looked over and saw Tim, Janet and Darryl all sitting on the bench outside Shasta. Christ, I thought, I look like shit. My hair's a mess and what the fuck is Darryl doing there? But this was the moment I had been pestering Tim about for three weeks. I walked over trying to keep my heart from coming out of my ears, mumbling to myself, "Here goes nothing" or "don't be a jerk" or something.

"Mitch," Tim said, with a Cheshire Cat grin, "this is my sister, Janet."

I smiled nervously and said, "Hi."

"Hi," she said quietly.

Then nothing. Total and complete numbing silence. A period of time that, in reality, lasted only a couple of seconds, but in the world I was currently residing in, felt like an eternity.

"How you doin', Darryl?" I asked, not really caring, but not wanting Janet thinking I only possessed one word in my entire vocabulary.

Darryl looked me up and down like he always did, which really pissed me off, then kind of gave me that "you're too late, asshole" smile of his.

"Well, I need to get to class … I guess," I mumbled. "Nice meeting you, Janet."

"Nice meeting you," she said, barely glancing up from whatever the hell was so fascinating on the ground.

I had blown it. That was my chance and I choked big time. "Just like always, you moron!" I castigated myself. "Just like in ping-pong, just like in everything!" Ping-pong was an especially sore subject for me, choking-wise. I had been playing Steve all year, probably four hours a day on the average and I had won a grand total of six games. I had lost somewhere in the neighborhood of two hundred-and fifty since we started keeping track. That said something about me. Either I'm very persistent and don't give up easy, or I'm as stupid as a fucking rock and can't take a hint. I prefer to think of it as persistent. Fortunately, or unfortunately, depending on how you look at it, I guess, I've applied this same principle to my affairs of the heart. I'm like a bulldog. Once I get a bite, I don't let go till you put a gun to my head and blow my Goddamn brains out. With Janet, I felt like I had blown my chance to even sink my teeth in.

But I hadn't. In fact, it was my teeth, or more precisely, my lips that gave me the inside track ahead of Darryl and Fats. Now I've always been very self-conscious about my looks. My roomie Dave was the kind of guy who could walk by a mirror, pause and then reflect on just how great looking he was. I, on the other hand, could walk by the same mirror and wonder where I got the doofy looking haircut. Or how come my nose looked like it had been smashed in with a two-by-four. Or how come my lips were so damn big! Peridontically-speaking, it was due to my Bugs Bunny overbite caused by tongue thrusts combined with what my orthodontist long ago called a short upper lip, whatever the hell that means. All I knew was that the only thing I had in common with a black guy, anatomically speaking, were my lips. I've always hated them, but I grew to at least like them when I found out Janet *loved* them.

Why? "Because they make you look like Mick Jagger," Tim told me.

"Mick Jagger?" I said disgustedly. "He's like only the ugliest dude on the face of the Earth!"

"Janet thinks Mick Jagger is the greatest looking guy in the universe …"

"Yeeech …"

"… and she thinks you look like Mick Jagger."

"Mick Jagger. Jesus, I don't even like the Stones."

Tim shook his head. "All right, Mitch," he said, gritting his teeth like always, "I'll tell her you're not interested."

"The hell you will!" I burst in. "Mick Jagger may be an ugly son-of-a-bitch, but if she likes him and thinks I look like him, then it's only rock and roll, but I like it."

"You are such a dork," Tim said.

◆　　　◆　　　◆

Janet and I got to know each other over the next several days, even to the point of conversing like two normal human beings. She was really a sweet person, except for the fact that she was neurotic in regards to just about every facet of everyday life.

"Want to walk downtown?" I asked innocently one day.

"You know, every time I walk downtown, I get yelled at by the homeless people," she said.

"They seem to bug me too for some reason," I agreed.

"I think they hate me because of my eyes," she mused.

"Your eyes?"

"Homeless people seem to hate people with pronounced facial features," she said. "My eyes, your lips, it makes sense."

"OK, um, how bout dinner then?"

"I … I don't really like to go out to eat," she said.

"How come?" I asked, having no idea what planet we were traveling to next.

"Because, I just think that, if I go out to eat, I'm going to dribble food, you know, down my chin and everyone will stare or laugh at me."

"Why would you think that?"

"Because it happens to me like every time."

"How many times has that happened to you?"

Janet thought for a moment. "Once," she answered.

◆   ◆   ◆

Time was really moving slowly, but in a good way. Janet and I had spent some time together every day getting to know each other better and finding out, just like Tim said, that we had absolutely nothing in common. Nothing. But what was great was that we were both willing to try the other's interest. I tried to get her to play volleyball, and she vainly attempted to get me to listen and adore the Rolling Stones. The first day, Janet and I attempted to play volleyball, a hard-hit ball nailed her directly on the thumb turning it eighteen shades of purple and ending her short-lived volleyball career. I kept listening to the Stones and came to like a majority of their stuff. It was really nice, but I knew that things were going to get scary real soon.

And I was right. It was on the night of May 10, 1979, three and a half months short of my twentieth birthday. Janet and I were in cellblock 110 lying side by side on my bed just talking and relaxing. At about nine-thirty that night, Dave came in, said his hellos and left. He returned about a half an hour later, and with not so much as a word, grabbed his pillow, his blanket, and his alarm clock and headed out the door.

"See you," was all he said as he left.

Janet and I looked at each other and laughed nervously. We both knew what this meant. Dave was headed for the study. Just like he had told me weeks before, he wanted me to kick him out, and I guess he was just helping me along with the process. But now what? There was this deafening silence that overtook us, seemingly sucking all of the oxygen out of the room. Finally, Janet sat up and announced she had to go to the bathroom.

"So do I," I nervously replied, and we walked out the door to our respective restrooms. The hallway was deserted but there could have been a football game going on and I wouldn't have noticed.

"This is it," I whispered to myself standing in front of the stall. "This is going to be the night. Shit. Finally! This is going to be great! Just don't blow it! She's done it before. Oh God …"

I looked at my reflection in the metal part of the urinal where the handle was. My nose and lips looked even bigger and fatter than normal. I looked like a cross between Don Knotts and a Gila monster.

I walked back to the room giving myself a pep talk. My heart felt like it was somewhere up near my left shoulder and my stomach was holding a butterfly convention inside. I had left the door unlocked so Janet could enter and be posing seductively when I returned. She wasn't. In fact, she wasn't even there. Now I really started to worry.

I waited. Not long, perhaps a minute, but long enough to start thinking she wasn't coming back—that good sense had overtaken her on the way to the can and she was now, at that very moment, pounding on her brother's door, begging for sanctuary. Christ, I needed to go to the bathroom again.

I stood there, hands gripping the sink like I was going to toss my cookies and stared at the little lost puppy in the mirror. Most guys lose their virginity in high school to some girl whose name they would forget the following night. But not me. I had one date in high school and it was a total disaster. I took Marcie Melcher to a football game and I felt like such a dweeb the entire night because I was so scared. I didn't say anything; I didn't do anything, for fear of saying or doing the wrong thing. The low point was when this little jerk who stood about four-foot ten, but whose parents bought him a yellow Camaro on his sixteenth birthday offered to drive her home. I wouldn't have blamed Marcie if she had gone with him, but to her credit, she didn't. I took her home, and kissed her goodnight like I'd kiss my grandmother goodnight. Then she stuck her tongue in my mouth and I nearly panicked and bit it off. That was the extent of my sexual prowess in high school. Now, there I was, about to go to bed with not only an absolutely beautiful woman, but a real sweet person too—someone I wanted to be with. Someone whose name I'd always remember.

I pulled myself together and went back to the room. She wasn't there. Shit. I walked out into the lobby. Nothing. I could see Dave lying on a couch in the study. If I didn't get laid tonight, I thought, he'll kill me. I went back to my room, sat on the edge of my bed and waited.

◆   ◆   ◆

Finally, there was a light tapping on the door before it slowly opened and Janet walked into the room like she was trying not to wake me up.

"Hi," I said, smiling and breathing a sigh of relief that could be heard ten miles away. She sat down on the bed next to me and we kissed.

"Are you okay?" she asked.

"Me? Yeah, I'm okay. How 'bout you?"

"I'm nervous." It was weird. I didn't for a second believe she was nervous, but I knew by saying that, she was trying to make me feel like I wasn't alone. "So, what are we gonna do?" she continued.

"I don't know," I said and kissed her again, mainly because I wanted to, but also because I couldn't get myself to say "Let's make love" or "Let's go to bed" or anything even remotely smooth. "Why don't we … uh … take our clothes off and get into bed and if something happens … uh … then it happens," I ended up spitting out.

God, what a moronic thing to say. I figured she'd get up right there, and with an insulting laugh say something like, "Sorry, I don't sleep with imbeciles." But instead, she agreed as long as I turned the lights off.

I was off the bed flipping off the light switch near the front door, and back on the bed before you could say "premature ejaculation." The only bit of light in the room now came from a lamp outside the hall that barely illuminated us through the blinds. I was out of my clothes, except for my underwear, in seconds. Then I sat and enjoyed the most beautiful vision I had ever seen.

Janet stood up and pulled her shirt over her head. I'm not sure she knew what a bra was, much less ever wore one. I could see the outline of her breasts in the soft light, my eyes getting more used to the darkness. Absolutely gorgeous. Then she unbuttoned her Levis and slowly stepped out of them. As she removed her panties, I slipped off my underwear. This was one of those moments when you want to be able to freeze time and step outside yourself to observe the situation. Maybe even take a few Polaroids. Janet's entire body from the top of her head to her knees was dimly visible, like in an erotic movie. Her face, shoulders, tummy; everything. As my friend Hank would say, "This is the kind of girl you write poems about."

I pulled the sheet and blanket back trying not to hyperventilate from excitement. I stood next to Janet in the darkness, wearing nothing but an ear-to-ear grin. I started to get in first, but she stopped me.

"I always take the side next to the wall," she said casually.

"Always?" I laughed.

"I mean ... oh, shit," she babbled as she climbed under the covers. I quickly followed suit and we began to kiss. Then I pulled back and looked straight into those big, beautiful brown eyes.

"Always?" I asked.

"Always," she replied.

We laughed.

13

o o o o o o o o o o o o o o o o o o o o o o o o o o o o o o o o
"Up on Chico Creek, they sent me ..."

—Robbie "Fathead" Robertson

There were several fine traditions that had been passed on through generations of Chico State dorm students. Most, of course, involved some sort of alcoholic intake, running naked down the hallways, and bad Elvis impersonations using a tennis racquet as a microphone while twenty other people stood around laughing at you as much as with you.

Well, at least they *told* me that was a tradition.

Anyway, the finest little rite of passage was "creeking." This was a wholesome celebration where members of the wing gather around on someone's birthday, sing happy songs filled with mirth and merriment then beat the snot out of him before tossing his lifeless body into Big Chico Creek.

My first experience with creeking a fellow "Freak" came with Gerald in 116. The concept was really quite simple. A group of seven to eight guys would gather round the room when the hapless victim was there. A little knock on the door, an invitation to enter from the unsuspecting chump, and then the bull rush. The birthday boy, Gerald in this case, was then to be dragged kicking and screaming down the hallway, out the door, across the lawn, past Lassen Hall, down the bank and then summarily tossed into the creek. All of this would be accompanied by plenty of cussing and followed by plenty of drinking.

Higher education at its finest!

It was actually a good thing to be "creeked." It meant that you were accepted as one of the gang. For example, Jim Hall never got creeked. Neither did the two loony birds in 106. And Steve never got creeked either, not because anyone thought he was a bad guy, he was just never in his room—he was always down in his girlfriend Beth's room on First West.

A couple months after we tossed Gerald, it was his roommate John's turn. John was another one of those guys that was always high, maybe not like fellow

Freak Kevin Simmons, who literally was stoned every single day that year, but pretty darn close. We all figured this one would be a snap. We'd bust in, John would say, "Dudes, what's up?" and we'd creek him with nary a struggle.

Apparently, John was not privy to our master plan.

Since Gerald had already been creeked, he figured he'd help us with John.

"I think he's probably too stoned to even realize this is going to happen," he said.

This was sounding too damn easy.

Gerald led us down the hallway and opened the door. There was John, face down on the bed, his surfer blonde hair covering his face, wearing nothing but a pair of white boxer shorts.

The group of us, probably six or seven guys, rushed in and grabbed him. Now John was a pretty big guy; big enough for us to know he'd put up a fight if he wasn't comatose.

But instead of fighting, instead of raising a hand to ward off this ugly mob, John reached under the mattress and grabbed the box springs like a pit bull.

Frantically, a couple of us tried to peel his fingers off the metal coils, but John's hands were locked around them like a chastity belt.

"John, let go of the fucking bed!" we all yelled in unison.

"Hmmmrrggghhh!" he grunted, his face buried into his pillow.

This was what it was all about, I guess. There was really no logical reason for John to carry on this way. All we were trying to do was wish him a happy birthday and show him how much we all cared for him by tossing him into a creek that, at that time of year, was only a couple of feet deep. Oh sure, he might hit bottom and the rocks might scrape away a couple layers of epidermis, but it was all in good fun.

The battle was becoming too much for us. Finally, Crazy Al, the voice of reason, stepped in.

"Just pick up the whole fuckin' bed and take him out that way," he said.

So that's what we did. Instead of trying to get John off the bed, we just picked him up, bed frame and all, and made our way out the door. We did have to turn the frame and John sideways to get him through the doorway, but after that, except for the additional weight, this was a much easier way to carry a 200-pound guy. We finally made it over to the creek and managed to toss John in, bed frame and all.

As the year went on, most everyone on the wing got creeked. Some I was a party to, other I missed out on for various reasons, none having to do with getting laid I might add. There was talk of creeking Bob McTine, the autistic guy that lived by himself in #122, but it was shelved because no one wanted to touch him for that long a period of time, and there was some actual concern that he might find a way to drown in two feet of water.

While John and his bed frame were quite the battle, it paled in comparison to the war that went on with Crazy Al.

This was a creeking that no one in their right mind wanted a part of. The fear, of course, was that Al would remember the names and addresses of all the participants, track them down, and pan fry their body parts.

"Hey, you guys saw what he did to that cow," said Feldman. "Count me out!" he said, waddling back to his room.

So while Feldman, his roommate Chris, and a couple others quickly made themselves scarce, there were still a couple of us around to try and get the job done.

Jim, Al's roommate and, as previously mentioned, a guy who used the word "fuck" or any variation therein in every sentence, was there. Gerald and John were there. And me.

"Let's fuckin' get him!" cried Jim.

"We need more guys," I offered.

"Who else would be this stupid?" asked John.

The answer? East Coasters. Or whatever you call guys from back east. Our wing had three of them; all with accents that were different yet sounded the same. All of them there on some sort of exchange program that let them go to a school 3,000 miles away in a town they never heard of to get an education that hardly measured up to Ivy League standards.

There was Doug, a nice guy from Rhode Island who pretty much kept to himself. I think it was because he had to be at least eight years older than the rest of us hormone dripping idiots.

There was Rick from Massachusetts. Lots of talk, lots of East Coast attitude all wrapped up in a guy with curly hair and about 40 extra pounds of baggage.

Then there was John Lorenz. Since we already had one John on the wing, he was simply known as Lorenz. He and his girlfriend Beth both came out on the exchange program from the University of New Hampshire, a fine little state whose motto is "Live Free or Die." We decided to see if that saying had any deep meaning to him.

"Hey Lorenz!" I said, banging on his door. "We need you out here."

"What's up?" he said, opening the door.

"C'mon, we're gonna creek Al and we need some help," I said as casually as possible, not wanting to tip him off to the possible death sentence I just imposed on him.

Now Lorenz hadn't been on the wing very long so he wasn't quite sure of whom everyone was.

"Is that the guy with the curly hair, kind of looks like a moun-kay?" he asked.

I stared at him blankly for a few moments, hoping an interpreter from the U.N. would suddenly appear by my side.

"A what?"

"A moun-kay," he repeated.

I looked back down the hallway, wondering if maybe Doug was in his room. At least I could understand him.

"What the fuck's a moun-kay?"

"Ah, geez, you Californians …" Lorenz started practically every sentence like that, but it was guaranteed if someone couldn't understand him or disagreed with his viewpoint. "A moun-kay … you know, an ape!"

"Ohhhh … a monkey!" I realized.

"That's what I said," he muttered.

"The hell it is," I replied, grabbing him by his arm and briskly leading him down the hallway.

The brain trust was gathered outside Al's room, giggling like schoolgirls at the fun they were going to have.

For some reason, at every creeking, one guy would always state the obvious before the blessed event. This time, it was my turn.

"All right, we knock, we go in, we grab him," I said. "Gerald, you and John get his arms. Jim, you get him around the body …"

"Fuck, yeah!"

"… and Lorenz and I will get his legs." I then looked at my dear east coast friend and very seriously said, "and Lorenz, make sure you grab the left leg."

"Why?" he questioned.

"Because, you idiot, his right leg is fake. It's plastic from the knee down. It'll freak you out."

Lorenz was stunned. "Seriously?"

John, Gerald and Jim all nodded in agreement.

"Well, thanks for telling me," he said. "That would've been kind of weird."

Finally, the moment arrived. The initial part of the plan, the part where we knock on the door, was flawless in its execution. Things pretty much went into the crapper after that. We went in and all latched on to our assigned body parts, but Al was so strong it was more like five fleas hanging onto a pit bull. Gerald and John each had an arm, but Al could still fling them about like rag dolls. Jim came in with a crushing tackle to Al's midsection that sent us all flying onto the bed. Meanwhile, Lorenz and I hung on to Al's legs like a pair of jilted lovers.

"AAAAAAAARRRRRRRGGGGGGGGGGHHHHHHH!!!!!" Al growled. He had decided he wasn't going to go down without a fight.

After what seemed like an eternity, Al began to relent. Not because he was tired, or because he couldn't have taken all five of us and mashed us into a pile of bone meal—but more, I think, out of boredom. And maybe the smallest bit of respect that comes from knowing there are five complete idiots willing to risk their lives to maintain a sophomoric tradition.

Once Al gave us the sign that the fight was over, it was easy pickin's. We carried him down the hallway, out the door and down the walkway past Lassen. Then up around the bend until we reached the edge of the embankment.

We slowly and carefully made our way down to the water's edge. Gerald and John, each still holding one of Al's arms, Jim holding the waist, and Lorenz and I each carrying a leg. When we were all in our proper positions, Jim peeled off like one of the Blue Angels leaving the four of us to slowly swing Al back and forth.

"Hey Lorenz," I said. "What leg did I tell you was Al's fake one?"

"ONE!" we shouted.

"The right one," he said. "That's why I got the left."

"TWO!"

"Oh. Because I think I might have that backward."

"THREE!!!"

And with that, Gerald, John and I gave Al a mighty heave toward the semi-raging creek. Lorenz was frozen, however, his mouth agape, his mind blank, and his hands, holding Al's prosthesis.

"AAAAAAAHHHHHHHHHHHHHHHH!!!!!" he screamed.

The rest of us were laughing so hard we could barely hear Al's cry.

"Throw my fuckin' leg in, Lorenz. It floats!"

◆   ◆   ◆

By the end of the school year, pretty much everyone had experienced the creek. I felt sorriest for the guys whose birthdays were in February and March because the water was running high from snow runoff and it was bitterly cold.

Being an August baby, I figured I was safe from all of this insanity. On one hand, it made me kind of sad to know I wasn't going to be able to enjoy the love and camaraderie of my fellow Freaks. On the other hand, this being late May, there wasn't a whole lot of water running and thus, the margin for error was small. But again, I felt safe since above all, the Freaks were sticklers for rules and the rules of creeking were very clear. In fact, they were posted in the hallway for all to see:

Creeking Rule #1: Creek a dude on his birthday.*

Creeking Rule #2: There is no fucking rule #2.

I must have seen that sheet of paper a million times yet for some reason, I never saw the tiny little asterisk attached to the end of Rule #1. Using an electron microscope, the kind the boys at NASA use to spot ice storms on Uranus, the small print at the bottom of the sheet apparently said:

"or whenever"

A subtle, but critical addition. If I had known that existed, that there was this time bomb of an addendum slithering its way along the bottom of the page, things would have been different.

There were just a couple days left till school got out. What had started as the living nightmare of a shy, scared out of his mind virgin, had turned out all right. Except for Jim Hall and the two weirdos in 106 no one ever talked to, I got along with most everybody. I had made some good friends, had some great laughs, and most importantly, was involved with the single most beautiful woman I could imagine.

I wanted to spend as much time with Janet as I could before summer break. Despite our myriad of differences, we had two things working seamlessly that contributed greatly to us spending a lot of time together talking or hanging out: Her complete paranoia over doing anything socially in public, and my complete lack of money that might have allowed us to do so.

So that evening, we were hanging out alone in my cellblock. Dave was off somewhere with Kim, and the rest of the Freaks seemed to be actually studying for finals or kicking back in their rooms.

At about 10 o'clock, Jan and I were interrupted by a knock on the door. I was wary because I had heard rumblings of trouble.

"Hey Mitch, you want to play ping pong?" It was Lorenz, my semi-understandable wing mate from New Hampshire.

"Ahhhh, I don't think so," I said, looking at Janet. "I got something else goin' on in here."

"C'mon, you beat me last time," he said. "I plan on skounkin' you this time."

Janet looked at me for the interpretation.

I shrugged. "You plan on whattin' me this time?" I said to the door.

"Skounkin' you."

I looked at Janet. "Do you understand what the hell he's saying?"

"C'mmmooooonnnnn," he pleaded.

Christ, I muttered to myself as I got up from the bed. I still had no intention of going to play ping pong, but I was getting tired of having a conversation with a door. And besides, except for Steve, I probably trusted Lorenz the most.

I opened the door and Lorenz walked in.

"Oh, hey, Janet," he said.

Before she could return the greeting, and before I could ask him what "skounkin'" was, the room was filled with Freaks. I had been set up.

"Wait a minute, wait a minute!" I futilely begged while my skinny-ass, one-hundred-and-forty pound body was being tied into the shape of a Rold Gold. "It's not my birthday!"

My protests were met with various expletives, none of which seemed particularly sympathetic.

Needless to say, the battle that ensued was nothing like the ones we had with John and Crazy Al. I was able to slip out of their grasp a couple of times as they carried me down the hallway, but the Dave put a vise grip hold around my stomach virtually squeezing every last molecule of oxygen out of my system. As they hauled me upside down out the door, I looked back down the hallway. There was Janet, appearing to be standing on her head, laughing and waving goodbye.

The trip to the creek was filled with laughter, joking and merriment—all at my expense, of course. I tried playing possum a couple of times, appearing to give up my struggles only to shock my captors with a furious two-second burst of super-human strength. All of which would quickly end when Dave would put the hammerlock on my intestines.

They finally got me down the bank.

"ONE!"

"You guys," I begged as they started to swing me to-and-fro. "Is there enough water in there? I mean, am I gonna get killed?"

"Who knows?" said Dave.

"Who cares?" said Crazy Al.

"TWO!!"

I looked at Lorenz who was holding my right leg, and appearing to enjoy every minute of his sophomoric revenge.

"Hey, Lorenz!"

"What?"

"What the fuck is "skounkin'?"

"THREE!!!"

I hit the water with a thud and in the process, imbedded a few rocks into my back as it crashed into the bottom of the shallow creek.

Eventually, I dragged my sorry ass out and made my way back to Shasta. I got the usual ribbing as I slowly, and somewhat painfully, walked down the hallway.

Finally, I reached my room and opened the door. I was stunned to see Janet still there, sitting on the edge of the bed, her big brown eyes looking at me and a big grin across her face.

"Did you enjoy your swim?" she asked.

I went over to her and she found a towel and started to dry me off.

14

"Affairs of the heart are like a tennis match. Love equals zero, everyone's got a racket, and the loser is the one with the most unforced errors."

—Fathead

The semester, which earlier on had seemed to drag on interminably, blazed by like a comet for the last two weeks. It figured. Just when Janet and I had finally accomplished the deed and were enjoying each other's company, it was time to say goodbye for the summer. I wrote her several times during vacation, but didn't receive one letter in return until about mid-July. We had talked on the phone about once a week, me at my parent's house in Westlake, and she at her family's home in Orland, just outside of Chico. Jan's family was pretty cool. Besides Tim, she had a couple of other younger brothers and an older sister. Her dad was in his mid-60s with this huge shock of white hair that he constantly ran his hand through while complaining about whatever baseball game happened to be on. Mr. Finnell had the whole house wired with a speaker in every room, including the can, so that no matter where he was at in the house, he could hear the Giants, the A's or whoever was playing.

So anyway, I finally got a letter sometime in mid-July. It goes on to tell me what a God-awful time she's having in Orland, sitting by the pool, drinking iced tea, and getting the shit bit out of her by yellow jackets. All standard stuff, including the obligatory, "sorry I haven't written" except she couldn't say it was because she was so busy. I took my own sweet time reading each and every word, trying to make a two-page letter read like *War and Peace*. Even though we hadn't seen each other for a couple of months, every word she had written took a mile off the distance that separated us. I really felt close to her.

Until …

"You're probably going to hate me for this, but I think that it might be best if we continue just as friends. I really like you, but I just don't feel like making a commitment to anybody right now …"

I took a walk outside and stood in front of my mom and dad's house, the same house whose purchase price cost me a trip to the University of Kentucky, and stared at the heavens.

"What do I do to these women?" I quietly asked. When God continued his lifelong lack of response to all of my inane questions, I walked back into the house, read the letter a few more times to make myself completely miserable, then folded it up neatly and put it in my desk drawer.

15

"There's no place like home, there's no place like home …"

—Judy "Fathead" Garland

A couple of weeks before summer vacation rolled around, Steve and I had a talk about our housing situation for the following year. Deciding to move out of the dorms and into some off campus housing really wasn't a tough decision to arrive at. When we added up all the benefits of dorm life, we came up with this extensive list:

1. Free toilet paper.

2. All day use of the ping-pong table.

3. Co-ed dorm made it almost like living with a woman.

On the negative side was a list so expansive that it had to be put on microfilm to save space. So we started perusing the paper in preparation for the following fall semester. It was just going to be the two of us. The fewer roommates, we figured, the better. But then Greg, the goody-two-shoes Catholic who wanted to be a rock-and-roll star, asked if he could join us so we said sure. And then there were three. Then David G., the psycho case with whom I occasionally played volleyball, joined the fray. Well, hell, I figured, let's just make it a party.

"Dave," I said, "Greg, Steve and David G. and I are getting a house next year. You want to join along?"

"I think I'm livin' with Stu next year," he said, referring to this dude whose brain was so permanently fried from drugs that scientists were baffled as to how he remained in a non-comatose state.

"You were supposed to live with him last year and that bombed out. What makes you think it'll be any different this year?"

"We've already found a place … I think," he replied with absolutely no confidence.

"Well, cool, let me know if it doesn't work out."

It didn't work out. So what started out as a Steve and I planning on sharing an apartment turned into five of the most mismatched guys on Earth living together. Sounded like another year of dorm life to me, without the free toilet paper.

◆   ◆   ◆

The house we found was a quaint little number on Sixth Avenue, right down the street from the hospital, about a mile from campus. Two big elm trees in the front yard swayed in the spring breeze, conjuring up images of lying in a hammock and virtually wasting ones' life. The house was owned by a fellow named Wilbur, a native Chicoan who spoke of "am-monds" not "all-monds" and who talked like he just walked off the set of the Andy Griffith Show. He walked us around, speaking highly of the large kitchen, the little breakfast nook "where, you know, you can eat cereal and stuff," and the four large bedrooms.

"Now boys," Wilbur cautioned, "the rent here is four hundred dollars a month and I need a one hundred dollar security deposit."

"From each of us?" Steve asked.

"No, just one hundred dollars total," he replied.

At that point, Steve looked at Dave and he looked at Greg who in turn looked at David G. who was too busy being a psycho-case to look at anyone. The same thought, however, was passing through all of our minds at once.

IS THIS GUY CRAZY?

Now I may be naïve about practically everything in life, but I do know that a one hundred dollar security deposit ain't worth a shit with five college guys living in a four-bedroom home. But we weren't so stupid that we were going to belabor the point, so we signed on the dotted line, handed him gobs of money, and left secure in the knowledge that we would not be sleeping on a heating grate come next fall.

That, we later came to discover, would have been an improvement.

◆   ◆   ◆

We all returned to Chico in mid-August when it's about a zillion degrees in the shade, the place is lousy with mosquitoes, and there's nothing in the way of a breeze to stir things up. Our little home was quite comfy looking nestled in amongst the large elms as it was. Dave set up the hammock first thing back and spent the week before the new semester listening to Bob Marley and downing sunflower seeds at an alarming rate. The rest of us patiently waited for our turn in the hammock by setting up what we loosely called furniture. The front door opened into the living room where we tossed this vomit-stained couch that we found at a yard sale for ten bucks, a plywood coffee table and my little seven-inch black and white TV. The interior decorator hadn't arrived with our collection of Renoirs, so I tacked up a couple of pictures of Cheryl Tiegs, one of which was the famous fish-net photo where Cheryl is wearing nothing but a couple of strings across her body, and you can see her tits from here to Nebraska and she had the nerve to say that she didn't know it was see-through.

Steve and I agreed to share a room because we were the two poorest sons-of-bitches on the planet and that way we could knock our rent down to sixty-eight bucks a month each. Dave, Greg and David G. each had to pay eighty-eight a month, and for me, those twenty bucks were the difference between eating and the not so delightful alternative.

One of the best things about the house we picked was that it was right around the corner from the house where some of our closest friends lived. Matt Bush had lived up on Third East back at Shasta where all of the quiet, studious-type people lived. Funny thing was I don't ever recall seeing Matt with anything more literary than Sports Illustrated in his hand. Also in that house was a guy named Steve Krzytowiak, also known as "Steve the K", "Hammerin" Hank Wilson, Janet's brother Tim, who continued to think I was an asshole, and Darryl, who also continued to think I was an asshole.

So anyway, with five fairly athletic guys doing fairly athletic things in one thousand degree weather, the need for more than one shower was overwhelming. This, we thought, was covered by the dual full bathrooms our house was equipped with. Once again, we thought wrong. The second day back, Dave, Steve, Greg and I went to play some hoops at the local junior high. David G. didn't go with us. Instead, he stayed in his room with the lights off and the stereo blasting one of his albums from his world-renowned "worst record collection on the face of the Earth" while plotting ways to get his four roomies to jump into a huge vat of boiling Wesson oil. David G. was one of those guys who had two hundred records in their collection, yet when you tried to find something to listen to, there was nothing good. It's like he purposely went out and bought the worst album that every major recording artist ever made.

So anyway, we came back from playing basketball hot, sweating, and smelling like the backside of a donkey. But fear not, we foolishly thought, two can shower now, and two in a matter of minutes. By luck of the draw, Dave and I were the initial victims. Dave headed for bathroom #2, the shower-only bathroom, while I went to bathroom #1, the shower/tub combo bathroom. The next few minutes revealed the vast knowledge of four-letter words that Dave and I had managed to acquire over the years. There was a slight problem when one of the showers was turned on. The problems multiplied when more than one shower was turned on at the same time. Those problems being:

1. A lack of water pressure.

2. A lack of hot water, pressure or no pressure.

3. A lack of water, hot or not, pressure or no pressure.

We came to find out that Wilbur had equipped our home with your standard five-gallon water heater. So after about three minutes of vainly trying to get my body wet, the hot water disappeared and the house reverberated with me and Dave's screams of "AAAAAIIIIIIIEEEEEEEEE!!"

After toweling off, the four of us reconvened at the breakfast nook for what became the first of many "summit meetings" to discuss the now obvious fact that this shower situation sucked. Of course, Greg and Steve felt it sucked just a little bit more being as how they were still covered in sweat like Arkansas hogs. It was finally agreed to by the four of us after discussing our impending class schedules and the like, that Dave and Steve would shower at night, and Greg and I would shower in the morning. David G. was not taken into account because, to be honest, we weren't sure if he ever showered to begin with.

The next few days before classes started were mostly spent decorating our own rooms with our own personal style. Dave went with the Jamaican meets white guy from the East Bay look. Greg decided on the "Father Knows Best-Donna Reed-Leave it to Beaver-1950's-A place for everything and everything in its place" ambiance. Steve put up his photos of Jack Nicklaus and Carl Yaztremski on his side of the room. No surprise there. I opted for a contrasting style: Sort of a "Spanish-Greek Goddess" motif, consisting of an old Santana poster and Sandra Joyce Cagle, Playboy's Miss February of 1978.

There was much to do. We had to figure out how to divide a refrigerator big enough for two pygmies into one capable of holding food for five manly men. To make matters worse, because none of us trusted the other as far as we could throw them, and except for Dave, we were all destitute, we each would buy our own milk and label it with our name. Invariably, one of us would leave a half full carton of milk shoved way in back for a couple of months, turning nature's goodness into a science project.

16

"What the world needs now is more love and less paperwork"

—*Pearl "Fathead" Bailey*

Things were strangely normal by the second week of school. Classes had already become a bit of a grind. My sex life was non-existent. I was flat broke. My bike was in disrepair. And to top it all off, my sex life was non-existent.

My heart was still in worse shape than the bike due to the "Dear John" letter I had received from Janet over the summer. It wasn't that I hadn't moved on somewhat in my quest to get her off my mind. Over the summer, I had returned to my job at Friendly Skies Day Camp and started dating a counselor named Daron.

Yes, Daron was a girl.

And yes, that was a major difference between Janet and Daron. Janet was a woman. Daron was a girl ... of 17.

Yikes!

Daron was a very sweet, very pretty, quintessential Jewish America Princess from Encino. Her dad was a dentist, her sisters had goofy Hebrew names (Ari and Schlee), and they were pretty damn rich.

I fit in like a Harlem Globetrotter at a KKK rally.

When I first saw Daron, I figured she had to be 18 at least. In fact, the idea that she was still in high school—a junior no less—never even crossed my mind. She just seemed far too mature, both mentally and physically.

So we started dating and it was nice. It got my mind off Janet, and gave me something to do and someone to spend time with during break.

But let's be clear about one thing. This relationship stopped at the waistline. Daron's young breasts were finally exposed after a while, but the best safe cracker at San Quentin couldn't unlock the shackle that kept her pants on.

And it was incredibly frustrating. After experiencing what I perceived as heaven, I was in no mood for a relationship that would take forever to consummate. But unlike Janet, Daron at least seemed to be committed to the deal and it was good to know I was going back to Chico with at least something in my back pocket.

Actually, that's really selling Daron short. This was a truly beautiful girl who probably would never have given me the time of day in high school. But here I was a couple years older, supposedly more mature—"not like the high school boys." I'm sure she bragged to her friends that she was "dating a college guy" and wait for them to "ooh" and "ahh." I was finally the "mystery boyfriend" that some dude in high school had to hear about.

And Daron would write letters, usually three to four per week. It was great to come home from class and see one of those pink envelopes in the mail. Most were just the usual crap about what had happened at school or home, but they always ended with her telling me how much she missed me and how she was looking forward to me coming home for a visit. I saved every letter and would read an old one when I needed a mental boost.

But I knew down deep that once I got back into town, I would eventually have to deal with Janet. My time with Daron had helped ease the heartbreak—or at least change it into good old American anger. I wanted to confront her, give her a piece of my mind, and then beg her to give me another chance.

The first time I saw Janet once we were all back, I ignored her. "Hah! Gotcha! Take that bitch! I bet you'll think long and hard before you mess with me again," I said to myself as I confidently walked past her.

I could tell she was stunned. Oh yeah, to most folks, the fact that she never established eye contact, or stopped talking to the guy she was walking with, might have indicated otherwise. But I could tell she was hurt. I went home later and waited for the phone to ring.

"What are you doing?" said Dave watching me staring intently at the phone.

"Waiting for Jan to call," I replied.

"You guys back together?"

Shit—way to ruin the mood. Back together. I guess that meant we were once together, but now we weren't.

"I don't know … I mean no … I mean … no," was the best I could come up with.

"I saw her the other day," he said. "She asked how you were doing."

That got my attention. I sat up like someone had just shot a jolt of electricity up my ass.

"What'd you tell her?" I asked, sounding like a prosecuting attorney, but looking like a beaten stray puppy.

"I said you were okay. Told her you had some girlfriend in L.A. that you met over summer."

"You what?" I looked at him incredulously. "Why would you tell her I have a girlfriend?"

Dave shrugged. "Because you do."

I closed my eyes and tried counting to ten, but only made it to about three or four. "She doesn't need to know that. Shit. Now I got no chance of getting back with her because she thinks I got a girlfriend."

Dave took a long drink from his beer, and then let out a belch that sounded like a cow getting an enema.

"You do."

I sat there, staring off into nowhere, shaking my head.

"Look Mitch, do you know why Jan hasn't talked to you since we all got back?" he asked.

"What are you talking about, I've been ignoring her."

"Because she knows she hurt you, but she doesn't want to be bulldogged."

"What the hell does that mean?"

"It means she would like to be friends with you, but she's not sure you could, you know, deal with that."

"I love her, I don't want to be friends with her!" I shot back.

Dave finished off his beer, grabbed another and started in on it. "That makes absolutely no sense."

"Shit … you know what I mean."

There was a long pause while I looked down at my shoes and discovered that each one had six sets of eyelets.

"Should I go talk to her?" I asked.

"Yeah, but you can't be a bulldog. You'll fuck it up for sure. You got a girl-friend, just remember that. Women like that—makes you seem more … desirable."

Well, there was a word I had never heard in descriptions of myself.

"Maybe I'll go see her," I thought out loud. "Maybe, I'll just … you know, go see her."

Dave looked at me with his steely blue eyes. "And no bulldoggin'."

"And no bulldoggin'."

A few days later, I was able to find the courage to say "Hi" to her when we saw each other at school. It was one of those stiff, uncomfortable conversations where each word struggled like a hooked salmon to come out. It was a lot of crap like, "how was your summer?" and "you look well." It was painful.

"Look," I said. "I think we need to talk but this isn't the place."

Janet looked down, then off to the side. All she said was "Mitch" in a soft pleading voice that begged me to drop the subject.

I didn't say another word—I didn't want to bulldog her or look pathetic either. I just stared at her waiting for a response.

"Tell you what," she finally whispered. "I'm living over off the Esplanade near Second Avenue. T-Marie apartments, number two."

"Just tell me when."

We agreed to meet later that week. I took the longest shower our house would allow before all the hot water ran out (four minutes), and then stared in my closet for the next hour looking for the perfect thing to wear. It had to give off a look, an attitude that I was searching for. It needed to project an aura of confidence and strength, while at the same time revealing the emotional scar Janet had caused. Above all, I had to look good in it. I stood there transfixed, hoping that Armani or some other Italian designer would pop out of the closet offering me a choice of his latest fashion. After what seemed like forever, I grabbed a pair of shorts and a tee-shirt with a beaver or some damn thing on it and headed for the door.

"I'm going to see Janet," I said to Steve and Beth who were sitting at the breakfast nook.

They glanced at each other with a combined look of disgust and sympathy. Disgust because their feelings about Janet weren't the most positive. "She's no good for you," Beth would always say. Sympathy, because as much as they knew down deep she wasn't good for me, they also knew how I felt about her.

"Good luck," was all they could say.

"I'll need it," I replied.

I took my time walking the four blocks over to Second Avenue and the two blocks up to the Esplanade. I tried going over every possible conversation ahead of time so that I could either dazzle her with my rapier wit, or make her cry like a mother at her son's funeral. I had put about four pounds of antiperspirant on before I left in hopes of not sweating like a nervous pig, but it wasn't working. It was becoming vividly clear to me why the stuff was marked down to half price.

I finally reached the T-Marie, and found Janet's apartment. I stood outside for awhile, wondering what the point was. I had a girlfriend who seemed to like me a lot, if not even love me. It wasn't like I was going to say some magical thing and she would say, "Ohhhhhh, you love me? Oh, OK, I'm sorry, I was confused. You bet I want to be with you." I started to turn and walk away, but something inside pulled me right back.

I rang the bell and Janet answered ... wearing a bikini. Not exactly what I needed to see.

"Oh, hi Mitch, come on in," she said somewhat embarrassedly I guess. While she ran off to put some clothes on, I quickly glanced around the apartment, looking for pictures of some dude or dudes as the case may be.

She finally came back and we started to talk. I don't recall a word that was said, but I do remember the feeling I had when I left. In essence, I was just a speed bump on her road to true love. I was like the squirrel that gets run over by a car. Janet was driving and thought she felt a bump. When she looked in the rear view mirror, there I was, floppin' all over the pavement, knowing my life was pretty much over, but trying to at least gain a measure of sympathy. But in reality, Janet didn't even look in the rearview mirror, and I was left to flop alone.

17

"It was a case of the blind leading the blind."

—Ray "Fathead" Charles

After my less than stellar reunion with Janet, it was clear to me that things were over between us, at least for now. Meanwhile, Janet began what I started referring to as her "y" phase—not "why" like in "why the hell is she going out with that guy?" but "y" as in "Billy," "Joey," "Tommy," etc., etc. Billy was the first guy she hooked up with that fall and surprisingly enough, he was my complete opposite. Tall, muscular, with long, stringy blonde hair, he looked like a harder version of David Lee Roth. I would see them occasionally around school and trying to be the brave soldier, greet them both as if I was so damn happy they had found each other. And Billy was cool about it. I think he knew the situation, but he also knew that my skinny ass was no match for his rock star looks, so it wasn't like he was feeling threatened or anything.

"God damn, he's a handsome guy," Matt would always say, often leading me to wonder about what side of the plate he was batting from.

But he was right. Billy was a handsome guy, seemed relatively nice and seemed to make Janet happy. Whoopee.

Anyway, I had other things to get to. One of the reasons I had left Cal State Northridge was because they had virtually eliminated student access to their campus radio station. What used to be a solid learning environment for budding broadcasters like myself, had morphed into a National Public Radio snoozefest.

I spent my first year at Chico trying to get my grades up, trying to grow up, and trying to get laid. I had actually accomplished all three goals to some degree or another. Now it was time to start working on life after college and what I hoped would be a long and very successful radio career. I had grown up listening to L.A. legends like Gary Owens, Lohman and Barkley, Hudson and Landry and Dick Whittinghill—personality-driven radio with bits, skits and unpredictability that made listening every day a necessity.

That was my dream, but I was bright enough to know that I wasn't going to walk into KCHO, the school's radio station, and be handed the morning drive time slot.

Not even close.

I had worked up the nerve to go in and ask what I could do to get involved with the station. I was directed to the stations' chief engineer, a sweetheart of a guy named Dave Talbot. He quickly set about taking me for a tour of the station, such as it was. There was the program director's office, the news room with the AP teletype clicking away, three small production studios, and the on-air booth. Right next to the on-air booth was the music room, a ten-by-ten area stacked floor to ceiling with albums, categorized from rock to jazz to classical. That was the thing about college radio; you got a wide mix of tastes to contend with.

All of this was well and good, but none of it had anything to do with what Dave had in mind for me. Instead he took me to what looked like a junior varsity version of the on-air booth. Stowed in a dark corner, the room featured a control board previously owned by Thomas Edison, and a stack of equipment directly behind it that included a couple of what appeared to be, prehistoric reel-to-reel decks. The control board itself had oodles of dials and buttons and switches. It had little red arrows inside of glass doo-hickeys that bounced back and forth like ping-pong balls. The bouncing arrows were obviously measuring something because there were all sorts of numbers directly behind it. Meanwhile, just in case there weren't enough buttons and dials on the control board, the big box of equipment sitting behind me was loaded down with more of the same. I felt like I was at the epicenter of not only KCHO, but all of international radio communication. I couldn't believe Dave was entrusting a newbie like me to handle all of this high-tech hardware.

"Mitch," he said quite Father-Knows-Bestly, "KCHO has the ability to broadcast on a sub-carrier frequency. Do you know what that is?"

Instead of showing complete ignorance, I related to Dave how it took me three tries to get my radio license.

"So you don't know?"

"No."

"Well, basically it works like this …," he said explaining a whole bunch of technical shit that engineers all think us morons just naturally know. I stood there looking interested, nodding my head in agreement, and trying not to pass gas.

"So what we do in here Mitch, is what is called the Radio Reading Service for the Blind," Dave said softly. "Do you know what that is?"

The old adage about it being better to keep one's mouth closed and be thought a fool, than to open it and remove all doubt, leapt into my brain, so I just shook my head.

"It's a public service we perform for the blind and visually impaired people in our area," he said. "We read books, magazines, etc., and it's very much appreciated."

"So, you want me to read something now?" I said. It didn't sound too exciting, but I had to start somewhere.

"Oh, no," Dave replied. "We have people who do that already. Your job is to run the tapes and monitor the control board."

Now, it really didn't sound too exciting.

Although being asked to "monitor the control board" sounded like pretty heady stuff, it really just meant watching those little bouncing arrows go back and forth. The worst part was listening to the tapes. Dave must have scoured the entire North Valley to find the most monotone, uninspiring readers. It was as if Dave and his crew were some sort of vicious "anti-blind person" cult, determined to make the visually impaired as miserable as possible. I could see them all huddled in the studio, their eyes bugging out while they plotted their evil.

"DIE OF BOREDOM YOU BLIND BASTARDS! HA, HA, HA!"

So that was my introduction to college radio. A couple nights a week, for about three hours a pop, I'd head down to the basement for another thrill-packed installment of "old, hacking, monotone, bore-the-fuck out of you volunteer reads the latest romance novel."

"Oh, John."

"Oh, Marsha."

"He grabbed his true love and stared deeply into her eyes. They were … (hack, snort) … blue yet in the moonlight seemed more hazel … (sniff, sniff, hack) … or maybe even green. She gazed back at him … ZZZZZZzzzzzzzzzzzz."

One day, I finally asked Dave if he knew how many listeners were tuning into our fabulous program.

"Well, there are over fifty blind people in the greater Chico area," he said.

"Right, but how many are listening?" I questioned.

"I don't know," he replied. "But we hear about it when something goes wrong, like when a tape breaks."

Just a couple weeks later, that very thing occurred. Halfway through a big sixteen-inch reel, the tape snapped in half like two-pound test. After watching the take-up reel go "thwip, thwip, thwip" for a while, it suddenly dawned on me that no one was calling to complain or at least wake up the board operator. Finally, the phone rang.

"Hello, KCHO," I said calmly.

"What the hell happened to the radio?" an irate voice screamed through the earpiece.

"I'm sorry, but the tape broke," I replied, again very calmly.

"Well, then fix it!" said our very unhappy blind camper.

"I can't, I don't have anything to fix it with," I said. "Besides, even if I did, I don't know how."

"Oh for Goddamn, Chrissakes! Jesus!! Then pick up a book and read something!" he screamed.

"All I have is my Poli Sci book," I said.

"Then READ IT!" he once again screamed before hanging up.

So I did. I began reading some chapter about God-knows-what and I had no idea if anyone else but that pissed off jackass was listening. But hell, I was officially a broadcasting fool. Two hours later, my voice was shot, my eyes were stinging, and my ass was asleep. Welcome to the wide, wonderful, exciting world of radio.

18

"Last night, it was so cold the flashers were only describing themselves."

—*Johnny "Fathead" Carson*

As fall descended, so did the temperatures. Things were staying relatively pleasant
during the day, but the nighttime temps were dropping like a whore's panties. It
was at this point that the five of us (Steve and I in particular), began to realize
that our humble place of abode probably did not meet the building codes of
Ecuador, much less Butte County. Steve and I first became aware of our particular problem early on. We assumed that our room was part of the original home
structure. Well, unless they used to build homes in Chico with Tinker Toys, we
assumed wrongly. One night, we were going to bed and I heard this scratching
sound on the other side of the wall. I let it go for a few minutes before getting sick
and tired of it. I pounded on the wood paneling that masqueraded as a wall, hoping to drive the critter away. It did—to the other side of the room.

Now this annoying little creature was next to Steve's bed gnawing and scratching away. So he pounded on the wall and a couple of seconds later I heard the pit-
ter-patter of little rat feet.

"This son-of-a-bitch is inside the wall," I said.

"Well, maybe if we keep pounding, we'll drive him crazy and he'll leave,"
Steve said, I guess thinking that rats use rational thought to drive their daily lives.

"Yeah, maybe. But if he can run back and forth from one side of the room to
the other—and he's inside the wall—that means there's no insulation, right?"

For once, I was right and Steve was wrong. Very wrong. The speed with which
our buck-toothed little rodent friend was able to race back and forth proved there
was no insulation, and perhaps, no supporting studs in the wall. Thus, my con-
clusion was deemed correct by an independent panel of judges. Steve's claim of
possible rat insanity being within reach was apparently not in agreement with the

rat's plans as he scurried from one side of the room to the other, giggling like a sixth-grade girl after her first kiss.

Finally, like two heavyweights who had pounded each other into exhaustion, Steve and I ended our pugilistic battle with the rat and fell asleep. The rat, meanwhile, skittered back and forth, no doubt dropping little rat turds as his own sort of "welcome neighbor" gift.

Night after sleepless night this little scenario played forth. The worst part was not that the little bastard was keeping Steve and I miserable each and every night, it was the fact that we were the *only* people facing this problem. Because our room was the add-on, it was the only one with fake walls. The other rooms in the house, those occupied by Dave, Greg and David G. apparently were built according to some sort of standard building practices. That extra twenty bucks a month was starting to seem rather insignificant.

It got so ridiculous that the other guys in the house didn't believe our tales of rodent interruptus no matter how bleary-eyed we appeared in the morning.

"I haven't heard them at all," said Greg, who probably would have had the whole town fumigated if there was something that dirty within eyeshot of his room. Dave concurred, but he was usually too high to even realize any of us were there, much less a rat. As for David G.—God knows.

So one morning, I'm lying in bed trying to catch a couple extra winks when I hear Dave start screaming a string of pearls.

"Get the fuck outta here!" he yelled. A loud crash, another couple f-bombs, and the sound of things breaking finally got me to stumble out of the room.

"What's the matter?" I asked.

Dave gave me the look. It was a look that I had only seen a couple times before and they each involved television specials about Charles Manson.

"There was a fuckin' rat on the kitchen counter the size of my fuckin' arm licking the shit out of your fuckin' grease can!" he screamed amazingly all in one breath. Dave could be quite eloquent when the mood hit him.

"See! See! I told you we had a rat in the house!" I said proudly.

◆   ◆   ◆

As fall turned to winter, it began getting colder than my love life.

"Where's the thermostat in this place?" Greg asked one day as icicles formed on his somewhat furry eyebrows.

"You mean the heater?" I asked.

"Yes, I mean the heater," he replied in his typical old lady style.

"Well, sure, it's right over … hey Steve, where's the heater in this place?" I yelled into our room.

"You're sitting in front of it."

Right next to the breakfast nook, attached to the wall, was this rusted piece of metal about a foot wide and five feet tall. It had some vents running about half-way down from the top and a little metal door that cleverly hid the master control panel.

Greg opened the small door to discover the master control panel consisted of an on/off switch and a dial to control how much heat we wanted blasting out.

A concerned look came over his face. It was the same look that would occur when one of his bed sheets wasn't perfectly cornered.

"I don't really see how this is going to be able to heat the whole house," he concluded after drawing up a couple of charts and graphs.

For once, I had to agree with him. It might do a good job of heating the breakfast nook, the kitchen, and conveniently enough, Greg's room, but as for the rest of the house, that seemed doubtful. The room Steve and I shared had an outside chance of seeing a couple of heat waves, but for the heat to reach David G's room, it would have to first get to our room, take a hard left down the hall, then a sharp right. Of course, David G. pretty much kept his door closed all of the time, so as far as we knew, he was already lying there dead as shit listening to some crappy record. As for Dave's room, no way.

"There must be another heater in the house," Greg offered.

"Or two," I added.

So we got up and did our best Sherlock Holmes to solve the mystery, but every lead turned into a dead end. So we returned to the nook where Steve joined us.

"Why don't we test it out and see what it can do?" Steve asked.

A brilliant thought, we agreed. Greg had the honors of flipping the switch on and cranking the power to full blast while Steve and I took cover so as not to be permanently disfigured by the intense heat.

At the flip of the switch, the heater began creaking, groaning and clicking like an old man getting out of bed. Steve and I ducked a little lower fearing the whole thing may just blow.

"Well?"

Greg held his hand up to the vents. He blinked a few times.

"Well?"

"Hang on …"

ZZZZZZZZzzzzzzzzzzzzzzzzzzzzzzzz

"I think I feel something," he finally said.

"You think?" I asked.

Further research determined that this little beauty of high technology was called a "space heater"—"space", in this case, referring to a three-inch area directly away from the vent. As winter took hold, a pattern began to develop. The first person up was required to turn the heater on full blast. This would allow the hamster inside to get a good running start on the exercise wheel that generated the power. Showers consisted of a relaxing two minute plunge into the water, followed by an Olympic qualifying sprint across the house to the heater. Upon reaching his destination, our hero would stand within that three-inch radius, then spin around and around trying to melt the frost that was already forming. Then it was another dash to the room for clothes and perhaps a quick jump under the covers. I was missing Shasta more and more.

◆   ◆   ◆

It didn't take long for the five of us to turn what was a reasonably clean rental home into the neighborhood toxic waste dump. We kept the outside looking decent by not throwing our trash out onto the front lawn like some of our friends, but the inside was getting worse with each passing day. Coach came by one day, apparently after swallowing a fistful of hallucinogens, to ask a big favor of us.

"Hey you guys, I've got a bunch of people coming to town and I'm looking for places for them to stay," he said. "You think you guys might be able to have a few of them crash here?"

"Who are they?" I asked.

"They're a traveling theater group for the deaf," he said without even cracking a smile.

"A traveling theater group for the deaf," Dave slowly repeated.

"Right," said Coach, shoving his glasses back up his nose. "They're on tour and a couple of my friends are in the group."

"Why don't they just stay at a hotel?" Steve inquired, no doubt in part due to his new job at the luxurious Holiday Inn.

Coach gave us a shrug and that look of "don't blame me, it's not *my* traveling theater group for the deaf" that we'd all seen countless times before. "They don't have a lot of money," he said. "They do all this stuff pretty much on a volunteer deal."

The three of us looked at each other still wondering what a traveling theater group for the deaf does. But it seemed harmless enough, so we agreed to let them hang at Casa De Waste Dump for a day or two.

The next morning, a group of about five or six scraggy-haired, tie-dye wearing, hacky-sack playing, kumbaya-types showed up. They threw their sleeping bags down in our nattily appointed front room without saying a word, then pretty much disappeared for the rest of the day.

"Must be doing the theater for the deaf thing," Dave offered.

"The *traveling* theater for the deaf thing," Steve clarified.

"So what do you suppose they do, all pantomime?" I asked. "I mean if the audience can't hear …"

"Is it the audience that can't hear?" Dave interrupted. "I thought they were the ones who couldn't hear. That's why I didn't say anything to them when they came in."

Just then we heard the front door close and Greg let out a muffled yelp. He walked into the kitchen where the three of us were, looking like he was trying to hitch a ride back to the front room.

"What's with all the sleeping bags?" he asked.

The three of us looked at each other. We had apparently forgotten to let our fussbudget roommate know of our freeloadin' guests.

"Coach asked us if a couple of his friends could crash here for a day or two," I said.

Silence.

"It's just a day or two …" I repeated.

Silence.

"It's only five or six people …" I said matter-of-factly.

Silence.

"… for a day or two."

Greg thought for a moment, his accounting brain cells calculating precisely how much of our home's natural resources this unwelcome clan would use before finally speaking.

"How much are they paying us?" he finally asked.

Dave kind of grunted a laugh out. "Paying us? To stay here?"

Greg didn't get the delicious irony, or the sarcasm, or much of anything to be honest.

"Yes, to stay here," he calmly replied.

Dave shifted in his seat away from Greg signifying that his part of this conversation had concluded.

"We're not charging them anything," I said. "They're Coach's friends and it's just for a day or two."

While that was certainly not the answer Greg had been looking for, I did earn points for tact and honesty. However, he was ready with more ammunition in this debate.

"What about showers? Have you guys thought about showers?"

Ouch. The three of us looked at each other in desperate hope that one of us had considered that potential snafu.

"I mean we don't have enough hot water for the five of us," Greg continued. "I don't understand how this is going to work."

Dave re-entered the conversation at this point. "You know, I don't really give a shit," he said. "And from what I saw, I don't think this group showers a whole lot anyway."

Steve and I nodded in agreement like a couple of bobbleheads on the back dash of a Lincoln. Greg puffed out his oversized bottom lip, pouting like a little girl and with a disgusted "whatever", went into his room to rearrange the molecules into perfect order.

The next morning, one of our new found theater friends asked us a question so shocking, so appalling and outrageous, that it left us speechless.

"Would you guys mind if I took a shower?" she asked innocently.

The room was consumed with silence. Various thoughts raced through my head; including, but not limited to:

1. There goes what little hot water we have.

2. She's not terrible looking, maybe she'll drop her towel afterwards and run around naked.

3. Let's see, the last time we cleaned the shower was … oh, that's right, NEVER!

At this point, we couldn't really say "no" to her, so we gave her the big A-OK and tried to mathematically compute how much hot water a woman her height and weight would use, and subsequently, how long it would take before hot water returned for the rest of us. Greg pulled out his mambo calculator that did everything but wash the dishes, and proceeded to do some quick computations while the rest of us stared on in breathless anticipation.

Suddenly, and without warning, a blood-curdling scream filled the house. The windows shook, the walls trembled and even our friend the rat scurried for cover. The four of us jumped up from the breakfast nook only to see our friend the theater gal standing there wrapped only in a towel. Her hair was only slightly wet, but wet enough to bring out a sort of Bundy-like evil in her glaring eyes.

"THERE ... ARE ... SLUGS ... IN ... YOUR SHOWER!" she screamed at us.

We stopped for a moment, then sat back down at the nook, relaxed and comforted that all was right with the world.

"Shit, I thought it was something serious," Dave said under his breath.

We all giggled like five-year olds.

"DID YOU HEAR ME? ..."

Was she still there?

"... THERE ARE SLUGS IN YOUR SHOWER!"

Dave looked up this time and spoke clearly. "You didn't hurt 'em did you?"

She flipped Dave the bird and stormed off.

"I wonder if that's part of their act," he joked.

19

"I don't believe in God, but I'm very interested in her."

—*Arthur C. "Fathead" Clarke*

My parents raised me to be a person with proper manners for the most part. I always did my best to say "please" and "thank you" when it was called for. I opened the door for ladies to pass through ahead of me, though most of them showed the gratitude of a prisoner of war. And I always tried to show respect for my elders. Even after a year and a half of living with these baboons, I tried to remain polite when the situation demanded it. This, in part, explains why despite being the least religious person I know, I always politely listened to those door-to-door bible beaters that would occasionally come to the door. Personally, I never understood the whole concept anyway. Why do these folks think that they might gain the complete trust of a stranger—so much that the individual would throw out whatever religious training they might have endured throughout their life to join the church that these two Stepford-like folks are pushing? And why do these people push it in the first place? Why do they feel a need to have other people believe what they believe? Isn't heaven crowded enough already? Won't more people simply drive rents up?

But anyway, despite my total non-believer status, I've always had a perverse interest in these people. I like to listen to their line of crappola and then have a harmless debate of the facts as I see it.

So one lazy weekend morning, there was a knock on the door and standing there were two of the sweetest looking little ladies you'd ever want to meet. They were both about fifty, both with round welcoming faces that had no doubt baked batches of cookies and attended many a church bazaar. I opened the door, and even though I knew what was coming, was polite as all get out.

"Good morning ladies, how are you today?"

Both of their faces brightened as they realized that not only were they not going to have to deal with one of those "horribly behaved college students," but that maybe I was like my dad's old '65 Plymouth—a convertible.

"We're fine," they said in unison, "how nice of you to ask!"

I smiled and asked what I could do for them.

"Do you have a personal relationship with Jesus Christ?" one of them asked.

"Noooo," I replied, "am I supposed to?"

Thus began what I hoped would be a five to ten minute discussion of religion and we would be done with it. The ladies kept talking about my spirit and my soul and how God killed his own son to pay for my sins, even though I never would have dreamed of asking him to. To be honest, I can't always keep the whole story straight, but either way, after a few minutes I was done with this part of my Saturday and ready to play basketball or do something infinitely more entertaining.

The problem, though, was those damn manners I was brought up with.

Every time I tried to give them the old "okay, well thanks, really appreciate it," they'd launch into a new offensive. They were like little General Patton's bringing their forces of niceness and goodliness down on my defense of "I don't believe any of this malarkey, but I can't tell you to go jump."

Forty-five minutes later—yes, forty-five minutes later—I was still standing there listening. The two women who at the start I saw as sincere, lovely people had turned into a couple of fat bitches at this point.

I long ago stopped listening to what they were saying, yet they still were acting like fishermen who finally hooked the big one and weren't about to let it get away.

Dave walked by a couple times to see what was going on, asking once if I was going to go play hoops or not. I gave him a pained look of helplessness, but all he did was walk away. I figured he saw me for what I was at that point—a weak-kneed, spineless, yet exceedingly polite, weenie.

As the fat bitches droned on, I felt Dave come up behind me again. This time, however, he didn't come empty handed.

"Did you see this one?" he said excitedly. I turned to see him holding open the centerfold from his latest issue of Penthouse so that both ladies could see.

"You ever seen a pair of tits like that? God damn, look at the pussy on that bitch!"

Then he walked away.

I looked back at the two women. Their round, pink faces had become pale. Their welcoming smiles had become disgusted frowns. But best of all, they were speechless. As embarrassed as I was, I was dying of laughter inside.

"Have a nice day," I said and shut the door. I had maintained my manners till the end.

20

o o o o o o o o o o o o o o o o o o o o o o o o o o o o o o o o o o

"Can't Find my Way Home."

—*Steve "Fathead" Winwood*

The end of the fall semester had arrived and with it, my first appearance on the Dean's List. Appearing on the Dean's List always sounded like a bad thing to me—like I was a hooligan of sorts that had stirred up a hornet's nest 'o trouble and was finally being taken to task for it. But in this case, making the Dean's List was a good thing as it meant that academically speaking, I had pulled my head out of the crapper and had posted a grade point average of better than 3.50.

So that was the good news. My evil plan wherein I didn't hold a job so I could concentrate on my schoolwork had paid off in clubs, if not spades. I felt much better about this whole "college education" thing and also regained a bit of self-respect after my placement on the Village Idiot list at CSUN.

But, as they say, at the end of every rainbow there's some poor son-of-a-bitch with no money. My unemployment decision left me broker than a five-year olds' toy on Christmas morning. I knew this pattern couldn't continue into the spring semester, but I had five weeks of winter break coming up to figure out a solution.

I was looking forward to going home for awhile. I missed seeing my parents and actually having a meal that consisted of something other than Top Ramen and hot dogs. I missed Daron, too. She had written consistently through the semester, sometimes up to three letters per week. And I had remained faithful too, which even though it may not have been completely by choice, was certainly admirable considering I was, according to the literature Dave quoted me, still in "the prime of my sexual prowess."

So I packed the Human Eraser with some essentials and said goodbye to my dear roomies and Chico. Greg asked if he could go with him since his family lived about 15 miles away from mine over in Newbury Park, so the two of us hit the road for the start of our ten hour journey home.

The first couple hundred miles went just dandy. The Eraser cruised down I-5 making relatively good time. We took a break to eat before continuing on our merry way. No sooner were we back on the road before visibility started becoming more difficult. A thick, low-lying fog had descended on the Central Valley and traffic quickly slowed to a crawl. Through the mist, Greg and I could see flashing lights in the distance: white, yellow, blue, red ... every color of the rainbow. We finally approached the area of all the excitement. Police cars had blocked the highway and were diverting everyone off I-5. A flashing sign indicated that all traffic was headed onto Highway 152 to Hanford.

"Where the hell is Hanford?" I asked Greg.

Not knowing, he rifled through my glove compartment looking for a road map. As we crept along the exit, I rolled down my window and asked one of the cops what was going on.

"Major accident down near Kettleman City," he said. "forty-two cars, couple tanker trucks. It's a mess."

"So where are you sending us?" I questioned.

"Got to get everyone over to highway ninety-nine. Five is going to be shut down for at least twenty-four hours, maybe longer."

"Found it!" exclaimed Greg.

Rand McNally had located Hanford on the map. It was, as we expected, smack dab in the middle of butt-fuck nowhere, a good twenty-five miles from where we were exiting the highway. From Hanford, it looked like it was another twenty-five miles or so over to highway ninety-nine. Nothing like a little fifty-mile detour.

To add to the joy, the fog had become so thick that it was nearly impossible to see the car in front of us unless we literally crawled up his ass. This is what I later learned was called "tule fog" from the ancient native American word "tule" meaning "can't see a fuckin' thing."

"How fast are we going?" Greg asked.

I glanced down at the speedometer. The indicator hovered just under the ten.

"About twenty to twenty-five," I lied. I knew if I told Greg the truth, he would have sighed, whined and complained. No way was I going to listen to that shit for fifty miles.

The Eraser, along with its two bored stiff occupants, slowly crawled across the vast wasteland of the Central Valley. Occasionally, the fog would lighten up a bit, lifting our hopes and allowing me to actually go the twenty-five miles per hour I had told Greg we were doing. But most of the way was a torturous, slow-moving, caravan of poor saps like us, just trying to get home.

Almost two hours later, we saw a light in the distance. Its bright yellow hue cut like a knife through the oppressive fog. It was the light of hope, the light of salvation. Like the Cape Neddick lighthouse guarding the rocky coast of Maine, its beacon guided us through the ocean of fog.

It was a Denny's.

We got out and joined the others who had silently and anonymously become our fellow road warriors. We sat down and ordered up dinner, since it was clear this was the only place for miles.

A highway patrolman sat at the counter, slowly nursing a cup of coffee while his radio crackled incoherently in the background.

"What the word on the fog?" I asked. "Is there any chance of it getting better between here and ninety-nine?"

He shook his head and told me it only got worse. "If I were you," he said, "I'd just forget about driving for the rest of the night."

"Any suggestions?" thinking that the booth at Denny's might not be the most appropriate place to bed down for the evening.

"There's a Motel 6 up the road just a little bit. You may want to get yourself a room and try again tomorrow when the sun's out."

Dandy. Denny's and Motel 6 all in the same evening. God's hand was truly reaching down and touching me on the shoulder.

So now our fifty-mile detour had turned into a fifty-mile detour *and* a fifty-dollar room. We choked down the rest of our dinner and returned to the Eraser.

"The cop said the motel was just up the highway about a mile or so," I said. "I think we should just stay the night and try again tomorrow."

"All right," Greg replied, "but let me drive."

I was going to ask why, but I didn't want to hear his reasoning. Once on the road, it became abundantly clear, however. The fog was so thick, we could literally no longer see more than a foot or two in front of us. As we crept along, it was painfully obvious that staying in the hotel was no longer an option. It was a necessity.

I rolled down the passenger window and stuck my head and shoulders out to see if that would help with the whole navigation thing. Other than getting wet and cold, and knowing how a dog feels, there was little to be gained. Suddenly, I saw a faint light off to my right. It was the motel.

"Turn the car!" I shouted.

"Where??"

"To the right, there's the motel!"

"But where's the driveway?"

"Just turn the DAMN car!"

So Greg turned the car hard to the right. We lurched forward as the Eraser hit the curb, and then plunged down a small embankment straight into a chain link fence.

"I don't think this is the driveway," Greg whined.

21

"Down, down, down with the Shah!"

—Ayatollah "Fathead" Khomeini

I returned to the Palace on Sixth Avenue in late January just days ahead of the start of the spring semester. I had made a few dollars working in a record store during the holiday shopping season, and had pretty much stolen every bit of food I could from my parents' house and crammed it into the Eraser to bring back to Chico. If I hadn't had to give Greg a ride back, I really could have brought back quite a bounty of chow. My parents, not really knowing my near-poverty like existence, and having absolutely no idea what kind of rathole I was living in, set me up with a case of Pepsi, a monster box of Top Ramen and more fat-producing crap like that.

It was nice to have a couple of bucks in my pocket for the first time in a while, but I knew that after a month of rent, utilities and the like, I'd be back to scrounging behind the bed for spare change. I knew it was time to get a job, but I had other goals for the semester, particularly at the radio station. After a few months of watching the tapes go round and round, I wanted to see if I could get on the air and really begin my career in radio. That was my top priority. I was in the middle of my junior year and hadn't really started on the whole career thing unless you want to call getting screamed at by crotchety old blind people a start.

So I needed a job, but I needed it to work around my classes and whatever the radio station would give me. Like a gift from the Gods, it landed in my lap.

There was a help wanted sign for an "information assistant" in the student union. What this position entailed at the time I had no idea, but the ad stressed "flexible hours" and that was enough for me to apply. I interviewed with a lady named Kathy and captivated her with all of my manly charms which basically consisted of a goofy-ass smile and half-way intelligent answers to her questions. She called me a couple days later and told me that she chose me out of seventy-five applicants for the position. If I had only had that kind of effect on women I wanted to sleep with, my college experience would have been far grander.

This was the perfect college job. My main duties consisted of sitting on my ass and watching people go by. Now and then someone might come up and ask where a particular group was meeting in the union, or where the bathroom was, stuff like that. The counter that stood between me and whoever was asking the question wasn't a barrier for me, but more of an icebreaker. Behind the counter, I was a different person. Much more outgoing, personable—not at all shy. I couldn't be. Who the hell wants to come up to an information booth and have to twist the idiot's arm to find out where the can is? So I chatted it up with whoever walked by, male or female, while all the time raking it in at a cool two bucks an hour.

I was working at the union three to four days a week, sometimes during the day and sometimes during the evening. The evening shift was good for getting studying done because absolutely no one ever came in to ask about anything. The day shift was a whole other form of entertainment.

Every day in the union, student groups of various sorts would set up tables so they could hand out their information to the students. During rush week, this was particularly big with the frats and sororities. But literally every week, the place would be filled with these tables and these student groups. My job as "information assistant" included taking reservations for table space from the groups as well as assigning those groups their designated spot. Simple enough, certainly not anything a relatively bright monkey couldn't figure out. But it was as an "information assistant" that I found a deep, dark evil inside of me.

It started out somewhat innocently enough when the on-campus rep for Campus Crusade for Christ came up to reserve a table.

"Great," I said in my most friendly, helpful, please don't banish me to hell for not believing in your whacko cause voice, "when would you like to reserve your spot?"

The perfectly coiffed fellow making the reservation politely asked for the full week beginning the next Monday. "It's our recruitment drive," he said, "sort of like the fraternities do."

Yeah, except of course for the lack of booze, drugs and sex, pretty much a carbon copy, I thought.

So I pulled out the big reservation book and looked to see what was available.

"Hey, you're in luck, I have one space left," I proudly announced. Then I noticed that the group on one side of the open spot was the Jewish Student

Union. Oh well, that should be fine, I thought. After all, religious people never fight about anything.

NEWS FLASH: RELIGIOUS PEOPLE FIGHT ABOUT EVERYTHING!

It was classic. These two bozo groups started arguing from the second they sat down next to each other and didn't stop until that Friday. People walking by would get involved in the heated discussion and I just sat in my little booth watching the fireworks and wondering why anyone was paying me to do this. By Wednesday, the folks at the table on the other side of the Campus Crusade group, who were simply trying to have a bake sale to raise money for their little organization, waved the white flag. That left me one spot in the union and if the prelude to Armageddon wasn't entertaining enough for God, he decided to drop one more little blessing my way.

"Hi, I'm wondering if we might get a spot in the union this week?" a gal asked me over the din of "YOU KILLED GOD'S SON!" raging in the background. She was not a bad looking woman, although she'd probably be better looking if she'd let her hair grow out a little more, I thought.

"As a matter of fact, I have an open spot right now," I said.

"Wonderful!" she replied, oblivious to what was going on around her.

"Great—and the name of the group?"

"The Gay and Lesbian Alliance," she said.

I smiled, rather broadly I guess.

"Something funny?" she asked.

"Oh no, no," I said. "Just happy to have you here."

But the centuries old battle between the Jews and the Christians and now the homosexuals was mild compared to one of my better arrangements.

In November of 1979, Iranian militants had taken over the U.S. embassy in Tehran and taken sixty-six Americans hostage. Now, in the early spring of 1980, those hostages were still being held and there was a lot of tension on campus between the pro-Shah Iranians and those that supported the revolution. Throw in the traditional Caucasian Americans who hated both groups and it simply added fuel to the fire. For the most part, the two Iranian groups kept their distance. It took someone with extraordinary diplomatic powers to bring them together so they could calmly and rationally discuss their conflicting ideas. Someone with a deep understanding of the history of the discord. Someone who cared deeply about the future of the Middle East. Someone like me!

The pro-Shah group came in one day to reserve a table. Frankly, the only way I could tell the two groups apart was that the pro-Shah group didn't act like they wanted to hang me by my testicles. Anyway, by pure luck the pro-revolutionary group came in later that same day looking to reserve a table. Must be rush week for revolutionaries, I thought.

Kathy had warned me that putting these two groups in the union the same week was not a great idea, but that if it had to be done, I was to be sure and put them on opposite ends of the hall to avoid trouble. I remembered all of that as this babbling fool asked for a table.

"I … we … I would like to purchase a … a … a … what you call … a … a … a … table, a table!" he blathered.

"You want a table in the union?" I translated.

"Yes, yes, yes!" he said excitedly. "We … I … want to tell college students about revolution!"

"Well, pardon me for saying this, but I don't think they really care about your revolution," I said.

For some reason, me saying that really pissed him off. He started screaming at me and telling me about how the Americans had done so-and-so to his shithole of a country and how the Shah was a criminal and a murderer and how the revolution would solve all of this.

"So if you're all fired up about this revolution, why are you in our country, you know, instead of over there helping out?"

So, maybe diplomacy isn't my strongest point.

Abdul was silent for a moment, except for his teeth grinding down to dust. He tried to calm himself as he slowly spoke.

"I would like to have a table. Are you going to give me one or not?"

I looked at him for a moment. He was clearly not interested in any more of my opinions. "Sure, let me see what I have available," I said with a smile.

I scanned the book and lo and behold, there was a table available at the end of the hall. There was also one available right next to the pro-Shah group. Again, I remembered Kathy's warning. She had said it wasn't a great idea to put them together, but she never said it wasn't allowed.

"Gotcha a perfect little spot right here near the front entrance," I said. "You should be able to get your message out to plenty of students."

Abdul took a deep breath and decided at that point to let me live another day.

"Thank you very much," he said, turning away.

So the following day I was fortunate enough to be working the morning shift when Abdul arrived to set up his table. He and his little friends were busy as beavers, or whatever fucking rodent they have in Iran, pasting up photos of the Ayatollah and a bunch of other guys that all looked exactly the same. About five minutes later, our friend from the pro-Shah group showed up. His name was probably also Abdul, but I'll call him Shahman to avoid confusion. The tension in the building immediately quadrupled but things remained quiet.

"Hi, you remember me, yes?" Shahman said to me.

After acknowledging him as a life-long friend, I pointed out where his table was to be set up.

"Sorry man, but that's the only spot that was available," I said with as much sincerity as a five-buck hooker.

Shahman turned to see Abdul and his cohorts planning their overthrow of Butte County and in the words of Rodney Dangerfield, was feeling no respect.

"I am sorry to be a problem, yes? But I cannot sit next to those people. They are …" Shahman struggled to find the right words.

"Horrible?"

"Horrible, yes! And I just …"

"Vile?"

"Yes, vile. And I just …"

"Reprehensible?"

"I don't know what that means."

"Forget it."

"Anyway, I just want to be far away from them," he said. "Why can't you put me someplace else?"

Shahman was quite serious in his request, or at least I thought he was. It was hard to tell since his whole face seemed to be covered in beard and moustache. But from the sincerity of his tone, I could tell that this was indeed a situation that called for maturity and a level head on my part. In the back of my mind, Kathy's voice once again reminded me of the hazards of putting these two mortal enemies within spitting distance of each other. The gravity of the situation weighed on my small, scrawny, underdeveloped shoulders. Fun was fun, but there was only one possible solution to this dilemma.

"Sorry man," I repeated, "but that's the only spot that's available."

I'm not sure if Shahman believed me or not, and frankly, I didn't care. I went back to my desk, sat down, and waited for the fireworks to begin.

It didn't take long. It started with a couple of dirty looks. Escalated further to what I guess was a string of obscenities in Farsi that would make a camel blush. A push here, a shove there, next thing you know, we got a whole mess of Iranians scrambling around on the linoleum and me on the phone to the campus cops.

"Hey, I think you guys need to get down to the BMU quick, we seem to have a small problem," over the bedlam that was ensuing.

"What seems to be the trouble?"

At this point, a stand-up guy would have accepted some of the blame and explained how he had miscalculated the level of hatred that existed between two Iranian student groups and had mistakenly put them next to each other in the student union.

"God if I know, but there's a bunch of crazy Arabs beatin' the crap out of each other here!"

22

o o o o o o o o o o o o o o o o o o o o o o o o o o o o o o o o o
"Want to Be a Rock and Roll Star"

—*Eddie "Fathead" Money*

Early in the semester, I had made a point of kissing up to the new student station manager at KCHO. His name was Steve Meeker, and when he wasn't completely stoned, he was an intelligent, mature and extremely focused individual. That happened once, on January 28. The rest of the time, Steve was just a really hairy guy with slits for eyes and a preference for the word "dude."

"So Steve," I said one day walking into his palatial office, "any chance I might be able to get an on-air shift this semester?"

He looked at me with glazed-over eyes and stroked his beard which ran all the way down his neck to his chest in a continuous manner. Man, he was a hairy guy.

"Dude, I don't know," he said. "When do you want to work?"

I saw an opening and I jumped. "Anytime, any shift, whatever you got. Just get me out of the radio reading service for the blind!"

He let out a laugh. "Dave has you doing that, huh? Dude, that's the worst. I remember doing that when I first started here." Steve thought for a few more seconds, shuffled a few papers around on his desk, and then finally let out the words I had been waiting to hear.

"OK, I think I got an opening for you."

"Oh man, that's awesome. When?"

"It's not an easy shift, but it's open."

"Cool, when?"

"I mean you do it for this semester, and maybe next fall we can move you to another slot."

Now I was really getting worried. As far as I knew, there were still only twenty-four hours in a day, but maybe in Steve's drug-induced world he had come up with some sort of parallel universe where days were longer and filled with horrible demons. A place where he could stick buck-toothed, no-talent radio wannabe's and doom them to a life of no sleep and few listeners. But I had said anytime, anywhere so I bit the bullet.

"When's the shift?"

"Tuesdays and Thursdays, twelve to three," Steve said.

Shit, I thought, that wasn't bad at all. I didn't have any classes during that time, and while I wasn't ever a fan of eating an early lunch, I figured I could deal with it a couple days a week.

"That's awesome!" I said quite excitedly. "So, what, I come on right after the noon news?"

Steve gave me kind of a quizzical look, like I had just given him a bag or oregano and told him it was Mexican Gold.

"Twelve to three … in the morning," he said.

"Oh," I replied, sitting back in my chair a bit. "Well, yeah, that makes sense. I mean, you said that it wasn't an easy shift. I thought maybe because I wouldn't get to eat my lunch on time. But now, yeah, that makes sense."

Steve stroked his Neanderthal features a few more times.

"So what do you think, dude, you up for it?"

"Midnight to three, twice a week," I thought out loud. "Let's see, I have class at eight in the morning Monday, Wednesday, Friday so that might be a little tough but …"

"Hey dude, it's rock and roll. You can play just about anything," Steve interrupted, noting that this was the only time of day or night that the station played the devil's music.

So after thinking it over for a couple more seconds, I quickly realized that staying up late in the morning playing rock and roll music was infinitely more appealing than watching tapes go round and getting screamed at by blind people. After the obligatory handshake from Steve, I was on my way to becoming the next big-time rock and roll disc jockey.

There wasn't a whole lot of time to start practicing. I sat in one afternoon with a guy named Jeff Pine whose voice sounded like his testicles were the size of grapefruits. His smooth bass voice explained in a slow, methodical way how to cue up the records, play the public service announcements, read the log and in general, do a radio show.

"So when do you go on?" Jeff asked.

"I think next week," I said. "Steve thinks he's got a guy to sub in this week, but then it will be my turn."

Just then, Steve poked his head into the studio.

"Dude, hey look, the guy I thought I had to sub in for you this week can't do it after all. So, I guess you're on tonight."

With that he shut the door, and probably ran off down the hallway giggling at how he had just totally fucked with the new guy's head. After thinking about how I had wished I had brought an extra pair of underwear, I turned back to Jeff.

"I think we better go over all of this again," I said.

I arrived at the station that night around eleven to pick out music and to get myself mentally prepared for my big debut. The record library at KCHO was pretty big, but it was mostly filled with jazz and classical music, which made perfect sense since that's what the station played ninety percent of the time. Its selection of rock n' roll was a little more limited and as I was quickly coming to realize, my knowledge of rock n' roll was even more limited. Dave had always given me a hard time about my Jimmy Buffett and Jim Croce records and now that was all starting to make sense. I had no idea who half the groups were or what their songs sounded like. I was starting to think that this was going to be the worst radio show of all time.

As I watched the clock edge towards midnight, my heart began to beat louder and my hands began to sweat. I kept rifling through the records, looking for anything that was somewhat familiar. Finally I hit the mother-lode—the Rolling Stones. My time with Janet, no matter how brief or how frustrating, was going to pay off because if nothing else, I now knew the Stones.

Finally, it was time. When the little red "on-air" light above the door to the studio flicked off, I walked in and introduced myself to the guy doing the jazz-fusion shift. He was a shaggy-haired dude, kind of like Dave, but he seemed nice enough.

"This your first shift?" he asked.

I let out a nervous laugh and replied that it was.

"You know where everything is, what to do?"

"Yep, I think I have that down. Jeff showed me a lot of stuff," I said.

"Cool," he paused for a moment. "You know how to do meter readings and then shut the transmitter down when you're done tonight?"

At that point, he might as well been speaking in Swahili because I had no clue what the hell he was talking about.

"Do I know how to do what and shut off, huh?" I stammered.

He looked up at the clock and then down at the record that was spinning on the turntable.

"You better deal with this and then I can show you what to do," he calmly said.

I looked down at the turntable and the needle was just about at the end. The second hand was approaching the twelve and I had not even thought what I was going to say when I turned the mike on.

"Better get a record cued up," he said in his laid-back style.

"Shit, shit, shit!" I grabbed the first record in my pile, but dropped it as I was trying to get the album out of the jacket. It hit the other turntable, causing the needle to skip across the top of the record like an ice skater at Central Park.

"Oh man, that's gonna sound like shit!" he exclaimed.

I finally grabbed the record and put the needle down on the first song. I didn't know which record I grabbed or what song it was, all I knew was that the damn thing was going round in circles and I could hear music.

"Why does it sound so funny? I asked, wondering why the song sounded like it was coming through Marconi's original equipment.

"Because you got the speaker in cue," he again calmly replied. "Right now, what you got is dead air."

I turned the pot up and just like that, there was music playing through the speaker system. I was overjoyed with a feeling of accomplishment.

"Congratulations," he said. He then had me cue up another record, put a couple carts in the deck in case I needed to play a public service blurb, and more importantly, take a few deep breaths. Once I segued into the next song, still too petrified to actually turn the mike on and say something, he showed me how to take the meter readings and shut down the transmitter at the end of the night.

"Hey man, thanks a lot for all your help. I really, really, appreciate it," I blubbered.

"No problem," he said. "I was in your shoes last year and someone bailed my ass out."

"Well, thanks again," I said before settling down in the big chair in front of the control board. I put on the headphones and listened to whatever the hell I was playing wind down, trying to think of something clever to say when I finally turned the mike on.

The shaggy-haired dude gave me a thumbs up and left the booth, but seconds later, I could sense he had returned. He was saying something to me, but with the headphones on, it might as well have been the Gettysburg Address because I couldn't hear a damn thing.

"What's up?" I asked as I removed the headphones.

"You do coke?" he replied.

"No thanks," I said. "I have some water right here." Gee, I thought, that was awfully nice of this guy to offer me a drink.

"No man," he said, holding up a small vial of white powder. "Do you toot?"

"Huh?"

"Coke, man. You do coke?" He was getting exasperated trying to give his drugs away.

"Oh, uh, no … I mean, uh … no," I said, suddenly sweating like a pig as I realized this helpful, friendly gent was probably a psychotic, murdering coke fiend.

"Cool," he said, and turned around and headed out the studio door.

I was still shaking when I turned on the mike and uttered the first words of my radio career.

"This is KCHO, Chico and um, here's another song."

I still can't understand why I never made the big time.

23

"Burnin' Down the House."

—*David "Fathead" Byrne*

While my radio career was now filed under the heading "Sucks, but at least Underway," my love life was not going as well. It was nearly impossible to maintain the long-distance relationship I had with Daron since we were only able to see each other during vacations. The one big advantage to having her as my girlfriend was that it spared me from having to actually pursue anyone else. It was a ready excuse for me to pull out of my ass when I would see someone I was attracted to. But in truth, no one, except for Janet of course, had really caught my eye, and she was persona non grata at this point, which is Latin for "getting nailed by some other dude."

Then I met Julie.

Julie Pearson was a beautiful blonde in my Beginning Production class. She had a smile that literally lit up the room and seemed like a warm, generous person. The first time I saw her, I was overwhelmed with her all-American, girl next door looks. She was one hundred percent, completely and fully out of my league—which of course meant that I had to ask her out.

Since we were both in the same class, and eventually had to do some work together in lab, it was fairly easy to get to know her. She was from the Bay Area and, of course, had the requisite mystery boyfriend named Bob. I didn't doubt for a second that she had a boyfriend, but I couldn't believe that this "Bob" character would let her out of his sight, much less head off to a college three hours away. After all, you never know what skinny-ass, big-lipped, doofus might try and hit up on her.

So after a bit of detective work, I discovered that Julie and Bob were having their problems. I figured that I couldn't just ask her out at that point, it would seem too crass, too insensitive. Not to mention that I was sure she'd turn me down flat. So instead, I put my famous plan B into effect. Plan B differed from

Plan A in several respects. Whereas Plan A simply required balls, Plan B required tenacity, perseverance and much smaller testicles. I tended to rely on Plan B a hell of a lot more than Plan A.

Plan B required a tremendous amount of patience and the ability to come up with ridiculous reasons to see someone. Julie had somehow managed to get a student-assistant job in the President's office so I would try and stop by to visit at least three times a week to show her what a swell guy I was and to frankly, wear her down so that when I finally did work up the nerve to ask her out, turning me down would be like throwing a puppy out into the cold.

The problem, of course, was coming up with reasons that I would have to go to the office of the University President. At first, I started with the old "hey, was just walking by and I thought I'd stop by" routine, but Julie along with the rest of the secretaries in the office knew that was simply a bunch of crap. My position as the information booth guy was good for a couple of visits as I created "important papers" that the President had to have a copy of—most of which were old table reservation sheets featuring my buddies Abdul and Shahman. Finally, I just shed the excuses and simply stopped by to talk and surprisingly, she wasn't showing me the exit immediately.

I found myself thinking about Julie a lot—much more than someone who already has a girlfriend should be doing. But since Julie was still involved with this Bob character, I figured I would just hang back and wait for the right moment.

Meanwhile, the boys of Sixth Avenue were beginning to enjoy the fabulous spring weather. The skies were clear, there was a slight breeze that blew through the big trees in the front yard, and for the most part, no one was burning anything.

I say for the most part because of one little incident that happened. It really wasn't a big deal, but it was just like Greg to make it into one. Dave had Stu and some other friends over one Friday afternoon for a barbecue and some beers. Totally harmless college fun—happened everyday on practically every street within a one mile radius of campus. They had their Bob Marley music going, a few burgers on the hibachi, that sort of thing. Finally, around ten, most of the guys went off to a party. Dave cleaned up the front yard, throwing away the cans and bottles that were strewn about, gathering the paper plates and tossing them into the trash, and dumping the used charcoal into a cardboard box that sat under a planter box right underneath Greg's bedroom window: a box where we always tossed the daily newspaper after we were done reading it—thus creating a cardboard box full of newspapers.

Did I mention the coals weren't completely cooled?

At about one in the morning, there was a knock on the door. Though still somewhat out of it thanks to the multitude of beers he consumed, Dave managed to drag his ass out of bed and make his way to the front door, stubbing his toe on the shitty little coffee table in the living room. Hopping and cussing, Dave opened the door, his dry eyes painfully trying to open more than a slit.

"What's up?" he asked the complete stranger who was knocking on his front door at such an un-Godly hour.

The guy hesitated for a moment, then casually pointed behind him and said, "Uh, your house is on fire."

Dave looked around the man to see that yes, indeed, the house was on fire. Not the entire house, mind you, but the planter box was definitely ablaze. Dave thought for a moment, scratched his head, let out a couple of obscenities, and then walked outside. The planter box that was attached to the outside wall of one of Greg's inside walls was now fully engulfed in flames.

"You got a hose or something?" said the kind stranger.

"Yeah," said Dave disgustedly. It was almost if he was more upset about the interruption of his nightly slumber, than the fact that his roommate was about to be cooked alive. He walked over to the other side of the yard, got the hose and eventually doused the flames. He offered a casual thanks to the man that had probably saved Greg's life, and in turn, the rest of our lives, and stumbled back to his room, once again stubbing his toe on the shitty little coffee table in the living room.

"Fuck!" he cried.

Wilbur was up early the next morning, rapping his wrinkled old knuckles on the front door. Greg, who was always the first one up in the morning, made his way from the breakfast nook where he was drinking some juice and reading yesterday's paper. This was perfect, he thought; he could answer the door, get rid of yesterday's paper, and get the current paper at the same time—a fine display of time management skills.

He opened the door to see Wilbur holding the screen door open.

"Good morning Wilbur," Greg said.

Wilbur smiled. "Looks like you boys had a hot one last night," he said wryly.

Greg smiled, but he wasn't sure why.

Wilbur stared at him, still smiling, waiting for Greg to respond. Finally, when he could detect no visible sign of intelligence emanating from Greg, he stepped aside and pointed to the planter box.

Greg looked at Wilbur quizzically. It was the same look he gave me when I had told him that I had no idea how to balance my checkbook. "How did that happen?" he asked.

Wilbur pointed over to the pile of ash that used to be the box of newspapers where Dave had thrown the now obviously still-hot coals, and the dirty little hibachi nearby.

"Near as I can figure, you boys had a barbeque that got a little out of hand."

The wheels of Greg's mind slowly began to turn. He remembered Dave's little get-together, and how he wasn't invited. He remembered the smell of the barbecue. Then his eyes got real wide.

"Dave!" he yelled.

We all came ambling out into the front room. Dave, who of course had suffered through a night wracked with guilt over nearly turning his roommates into Kingsford briquettes, was last to arrive. Greg was as mad as I had ever seen him. His puffy lips were trembling and it looked like he was either going to explode in a fury of rage, or cry like a seven-year old girl.

"God damnit Dave, you almost burned the fucking house down!" he screamed.

It was now clear that Greg was not going to cry like a seven-year old girl. I had never heard him cuss like that before and I think even Dave knew that maybe, just maybe, he had screwed up.

"Now boys," Wilbur said, trying to bring peace to the family, "I don't want you get too upset about all of this."

Greg was shooting a laser look at Dave. "You're paying for the damage!" he said sternly.

Dave had no choice. It was clearly his fault and no amount of fast talking or charm was going to get him out of this one.

"Wilbur, I guess the coals weren't out when I threw them in the box last night, I'm real sorry," he said with a hangdog look.

"Well, I understand this sort of thing happens …"

Steve and I looked at each other. This sort of thing happens? How many times in the past have your tenants thrown hot coals into a cardboard box full of newspaper and then been woken up in the middle of the night to be told the house was on fire?

"How much am I going to owe you?" Dave asked.

"Well," Wilbur thought. "It certainly could have been a lot worse. The planter box is pretty well shot."

"Well, technically Wilbur, there were no plants in it," interjected Dave.

"Shut up, Dave!" Greg said.

Wilbur rubbed his wrinkly chin and surveyed the damage one more time. Then he gave Dave a serious look. "You know, Dave, this could have been a very serious incident. You're awfully lucky that nothing worse happened." He pondered his next thought like a Supreme Court justice deciding on a life or death sentence.

"I'm afraid I'm going to have to charge you twenty dollars to fix the damage," he finally said.

Greg was dumbfounded. "Wilbur, are you out of your mind?" he said incredulously.

Wilbur looked at him like a more than disappointed father.

"Now, Greg, there really wasn't that much damage—it was just the planter box," he said sternly.

"But he could have burned the whole house down, not to mention killing all of us!"

"And it's my house," continued Wilbur. Greg and Wilbur then began the day's staring contest which lasted about five seconds before Greg blinked.

"Awww," Greg whined turning around in disgust.

Dave wasn't stupid enough to argue the point. "Twenty bucks it is," he said and went back to his room to pry a Jackson away from his drug stash. He returned to the front room and gave Steve and I a satisfied look, then handed the twenty to Wilbur.

"Again, Wilbur, I'm real sorry this happened," he said contritely. "It'll never happen again."

Wilbur smiled and let out a little chuckle. "I know it won't, Dave, but if it does, then I'm going to charge you forty dollars, and I think Greg may kill you."

And with that, he folded the twenty up, put it in his pocket, turned and walked away.

24

"A relationship, I think, is like a shark. It has to constantly move forward or it dies. And I think what we got on our hands is a dead shark."

—*Woody "Fathead" Allen*

Summer finally came and not a moment too soon. I was horny as ever and for some reason, I was convinced that once I got home, Daron would be almost begging me to rip her clothes off.

We both started working at the day camp again where we had met each other the previous summer. I was happy to be back working with the kids and the counselors, and happy to be able to see Daron. Things were going to be great, I thought.

But it wasn't. Daron had changed, which is of course, understandable. She seemed not exactly cold, but certainly not warm—more like disinterested. It was as if having a relationship with a guy away at college was cool, and made her feel cool in front of her friends; but once the reality of the guy coming home occurred, the whole coolness factor flew out the window.

We went out to dinner one night early in the summer and it was a battle to get her to have a conversation. Something was definitely on her mind, but I had no clue that the hammer was coming down momentarily.

"So what's going on, you're so quiet tonight," I said in between bites.

She shook her head and sighed.

"What is it? What's wrong?"

She took a deep breath, closed her eyes, and then let out a big exhale. Then she said the four words that no man ever wants to hear. The four words that throughout history have only meant doom, destruction and sometimes death. The four words that have brought empires crashing down in an avalanche of misery and despair. The four words that were going to break my heart once again.

"We need to talk."

I could feel the knife go into my heart and Daron's hand twisting it around and around like a carousel. There was no mistaking it. She wasn't going to talk about the weather or how the Dodgers were doing. She was going to take my right ventricle, tie it in a nice bow, then run my left ventricle through it and winch it tight like a trucker carrying a load of lumber.

"I just think it's time we stop seeing each other," she said softly.

I was dumbfounded, which really shouldn't have been a surprise since I've never been too good at cluing in on the obvious. I asked her what I had done wrong and where did I screw up—the usual questions a guy begging to still be loved would ask.

"It's nothing you've done," she said, practically reading from the book entitled *How to Break Up with a Loser,* "it's me."

I thought for a moment. We were in a nice restaurant so I couldn't exactly lose my cool and start screaming and yelling, or worse blubbering like a four-year old. Then it hit me—she didn't want to break up with me at all. She was being forced to by her parents. I knew they had it in for me from the start.

"It's your parents isn't it?" I asked.

"What do you mean?"

"I'm not Jewish enough for them," I replied. "The only reason they let you date me at all was because they knew my mom was sort of Jewish so they probably figured there was hope for me. But once I screwed up the Sader dinner and, oh shit, that's right, they saw me going into McDonald's on Passover ..." I knew at that point I had hit it on the head. I just kind of started laughing and saying "I'm not Jewish enough, that's it, I'm not Jewish enough!"

"You're crazy," Daron said, "it has nothing to do with that."

"Bull!" I yelled. Now I was mad. I was mad at Daron, and I was mad at her parents, and I was mad because I knew I probably wasn't ever going to see this beautiful girl again.

"I'm sorry," she kept saying over and over, but my anger was just growing and growing. All I wanted to do was get the hell out of there at that point, so I threw enough money on the table to cover our dinners and tip, got up and walked out.

Daron came running after me. "Look, just calm down, all right?"

I wasn't listening to her.

"Just take me home and we can talk about things tomorrow when you've cooled off," she said.

I turned around and glared at her. "You think I'm going to be cooled off by tomorrow? Are you crazy?" I was livid by that point and I could see in Daron's eyes that she knew it. "I'm not going to get over this by tomorrow!"

The drive back to her house was silent and easily the longest 15 minutes of our lives. I pulled into the circular driveway in front of her parent's Encino home. I wanted so much to go knock on the door and tell her mom and dad what a bunch of crap this whole thing was and that because of them, their daughter was missing out on a good guy. But instead I just stared straight ahead.

"I'm sorry," Daron said for the two thousandth time, as she wiped a tear away.

"I'm sorry too," was all I could say.

"I hope we can still be friends," she said as she climbed out of the car. "I don't want to lose your friendship."

I laughed. I thought about how it had always seemed absurd to me that two people can be in love with each other one minute, break up, and hate each other the next minute. It seemed like the logical next step would be friendship, I mean after all, that's probably how the whole damn relationship started in the first place. But it never worked out like that. Two people break up, they usually cut the cord for good. There's just no going back.

"Sure," I lied. "We can still be friends."

◆   ◆   ◆

With Daron now taking herself out of the picture, and after the requisite amount of "I hate all women" time having passed, I was able to start thinking about Julie again. The fall semester of my senior year arrived soon enough and I knew that I had to have more of a plan than simply wearing her down until she begged me to take her out rather than go through another day of torture.

My opportunity to ask her out presented itself late one night early in September. We were taking an Advanced Radio Production class together and we had a fairly major project to work on. We were down in the KCHO studios late at night along with a few other students from class and a guy named Carl Bloch. Carl was considered a rarity at Chico State since he was … black. There simply weren't a whole lot of brothers in Butte County so getting black students to come up from L.A. or the San Francisco Bay area had been an ongoing problem for the administration. Recruiting slogans like "Chico—It's Way Better than Oakland" and "Chico—It Isn't Just for White Folks Anymore" just weren't cutting it.

Julie and I had done all of our weeks of flirting the previous spring and into the fall and absolutely nothing was happening because, as per usual, I was too petrified to make any sort of move. Carl and I had talked in the past about it so he was using this opportunity to ride my ass to no end.

"You just got to ask her out for a drink or something," he said to me that night. "C'mon man, she digs you, I can tell. Just do it!"

Carl had his shit-eatin' grin on his face so I couldn't tell if he was telling me the truth or at least what he thought was the truth, or simply bullshitting me.

I was looking at Julie doing some work in studio B. She so friggin' beautiful, I thought, there is no way she'll go out with me.

"I don't know man," I said. "She's out of my league."

"Bullshit!" Carl said. He paused for a moment to collect his thoughts. "Look man, here's the thing," he said softly. "If you don't ask her out, I will."

"You?" I said. "You're going to ask out Julie?"

"Why, what's wrong with that? You don't think she'd go for me? Why, because I'm black? I don't think so baby. She'd go for me because I'm black! In fact, fuck you; I'm going to ask her out right now!"

I put my hand firmly on his shoulder to stop him from heading to studio B and perhaps making a fool of himself. Or maybe it was because I figured he would do it and he'd be right; Julie would be all for it and once again, I'd be on the outside looking in.

At that moment, Julie came out of the studio and asked what was going on.

I stared at Carl for a second, with a half worried, half threatening glance. He just smiled and said we were talking about what we were going to do on the weekend.

"What about you, Julie? What you got goin' on this weekend?" he smirked.

"Not much, probably be down here again finishing off this stupid project. I'd like to go out at least one night."

Carl glared at me. His eyes simply bore through my skull and into my brain transmitting the message "TAKE THE HINT, MORON!"

"Mitch?" he said slowly.

I could feel my whole body begin to sweat and my heart begin to pound like a conga drum. I knew what to say but I couldn't get my brain and my mouth on the same page. I was dying a slow, painful death and Carl was deciding whether or not to throw me a lifeline.

"Hey, let's see what's playing at the midnight movie tonight," he said, grabbing one of the student newspapers that were left in a stack in the studio. It seemed that Julie was completely oblivious to my suffering which was all-in-all a good thing.

Carl flipped through the pages until he found the movie section.

"Please don't tell me it's the *Rocky Horror Picture Show*," I begged, recalling my horrific first midnight movie experience. Since that alcohol saturated evening, the only time I'd been to the midnight movie at El Rey was when the Freaks went to watch the occasional X-rated flick.

"Nope, looks like it's *A Clockwork Orange*."

"Really? I've kind of always wanted to see that movie," I said.

Julie nodded in agreement. "Yeah, me too. I've heard a lot about it, but I've never seen it."

Then there was a long, long pause. In the background, I could hear the soft sounds of the other students, an occasional laugh, a door closing. I could also hear the deafening silence that surrounded the three of us. I looked down at my feet, hoping that perhaps I had written a witty line on my sneakers before I left the house, but once again, my inability to predict the future cost me.

Finally, Carl couldn't stand it anymore. "Sounds like both of you guys want to see that movie. Why don't you pack it up for the night and do it?"

Yeah, I thought, nodding at Julie, what he said.

Julie brightened. "Sounds like a good idea to me ..."

YES! YES! YES! I thought.

"You should come with us," she said cheerfully.

NO! NO! NO! I thought.

Carl looked at me and smiled, his pearly white teeth shining brightly through his full beard.

"That sounds like fun," he said.

I glared at him trying to mentally transmit the message that I was very close to several white supremacist groups in the area and I would have no hesitation about calling them out to beat his black ass to a pulp.

"But I got to get up real early in the morning," he continued, apparently receiving my hate-mail message loud and clear. "You two should just go."

I looked at Julie, fully expecting her to say she just remembered her cat was home sick and she'd have to take a pass. But miraculously, she instead agreed to accompany me for the evening.

We strolled over to the El Rey through the warm evening air, talking and laughing. I had finally relaxed by approaching this as just as couple of friends going to a movie instead of thinking about what an absolute babe I was with. We made our way through the lobby and found a couple of seats midway up the aisle. The movie was going to begin in just a couple of minutes, so I offered to run up and get us some popcorn and drinks. Julie was all for that, so I ambled back to the lobby and got in what was later officially named, the "World's Longest, Slowest, Fucking Line in the History of Movie Theaters. Ever."

So I'm standing in the WLSFLHMTE with the other poor bastards waiting to spend what little money I actually had on cold popcorn and a flat soda. But, I was excited as all hell because Julie and I were out on a date, even if she didn't see it that way. I was still a good five or six people from the counter when I could hear music coming from inside the theater. That's okay, I thought to myself, they always show about ten minutes of previews before the movie actually starts. I'll be back to my seat before the whole deal begins.

Meanwhile, the stoned out numbskulls ahead of me were staring at the menu trying to decide what to order. "It's a fucking movie theater," I mumbled, "they got popcorn, soda and maybe an old hot dog. Just fucking order something." Meanwhile, in the theater, the music had changed. And next to me, a guy started bouncing up and down like he had to piss like a Russian racehorse.

"Damn it, damn it, damn it!" he cried.

I looked over at him with a slight bit of concern. "What's the problem?"

"Aw man, that's the beginning of the movie," he whined, trying to look past the others in front of him in line.

"It'll just be the opening credits, no big deal," I offered.

He looked at me like I had just landed on Earth from the planet Zoltorb.

"I've seen this flick probably a dozen times," he said in a deadly serious manner. "If you miss the beginning, you might as well miss the whole fucking movie."

"Why?"

"Why? Why? Because there's like this great rape scene right at the start! These guys break into a house and kick the living shit out of this old dude then tear the clothes off this chick and then rape her all while dancing to "Singing in the Rain. It's awesome!"

I looked at this goofball and wondered how the hell we were considered part of the same species. But in my mind, the only thought I had was that this was probably not the best choice for a first date movie.

The line slowly inched forward and our coked out pal was getting more and more agitated. Meanwhile, in the background, the music had stopped only to be replaced by the muffled sounds of screaming and crashing.

"God damn it!" he blurted out.

There were still two people in front of me when I could hear the beginnings of one of the finest, most enjoyable and happy songs ever to come out of the movie industry.

"I'm singing in the rain … ummph!"

"Awww man," said our friend, as the aneurysm exploded inside his brain.

Finally, I got to the counter, ordered the crap and ran back to my seat. There was Julie, her eyes as big as one of them funny-looking fish that live at the bottom of the ocean—the ones that never see any light. Her mouth was agape, and the rest of her face had a general look of horror to it.

"Did I miss anything?" I whispered innocently as I sat down next to her.

Julie didn't say anything for a second. Then she finally spoke slowly. "They showed everything ... everything."

◆   ◆   ◆

Despite taking her to a great "rape movie" for our first "date," Julie agreed to go out on a real life date a few days later. Well, actually, our date consisted of me going over to her house for dinner and watching an old movie on TV. Her house was a classic Chico arts-and-crafts style home on Second Avenue on the good side of the Esplanade. It was the good side because it wasn't the area where most of the students lived. Julie lived in a little yellow house with a couple other girls, who fortunately were gone for the evening.

Anyway, we had burgers or something, then planted ourselves on the couch a good couple of feet away from each other. Julie was a big fan of old black and white movies, and as we watched this old fashioned story of romance and intrigue, I couldn't help but think about what a fine choice "A Clockwork Orange" had been.

"Boy, that was some movie we saw the other night," I said for some reason.

"Yeah, I'm not sure that's one I would want to see again," she said in the most gigantic of understatements.

"Yeah," I cleverly replied.

Suddenly, Julie grabbed a pillow that had been sitting on top of the couch, put it on my lap, and laid down with her head on the pillow. In other words, her head was practically in my lap, sans a few inches of polyester and acrylic cotton separation. I tried to act like it was nothing—like it was a totally natural thing to have happened. Meanwhile, my brain was going a million miles an hour, mostly focusing on two separate yet equal thoughts:

Don't fart. Don't cum in your pants.

I finally got the nerve to put my hand on her shoulder and gently rub her upper right arm. Julie was wearing a black and red flannel shirt that was as soft to the touch as I imagined her skin to be. Looking back at me, she appeared to have somehow arranged for some Hollywood backlighting because even in the dimly lit house, she glowed. Her face, softened by the light like one of the actresses we were watching in the old movie, was as beautiful as any I had ever seen. She smiled slightly and I leaned down to kiss her.

"Do you think this is the right thing to do?" she asked. "I don't want to ruin our friendship."

"Trust me, this will not ruin our friendship," I said.

When we had first met, I had set a goal to go out on at least one date with Julie. When that happened, my goal changed. My goal then became to kiss her at least once. Now that had occurred and my goal was going to change again.

We watched the movie till the bitter end, though I had long ago stopped paying attention to what was going on. My brain cells were working overtime reviewing, analyzing and deconstructing the entire scene that led to our first kiss. Julie got up to turn the TV off then turned to me.

"Do you want to stay here tonight?" she asked somewhat hesitantly.

After approximately one-half a millisecond of thought I replied that I would.

"Okay," she said before going into her bedroom and coming out with a couple pillows and an old blanket. "Do you want to sleep on the couch or the bed?" she asked.

With that, my dream of achieving my final goal exploded in a cascade of disappointment and cheap linens. How the hell did I misread that signal, I thought. Good God, when someone asks someone else if they want to stay the night, isn't that normally considered an E ticket to the Pleasuredome? Now I was stuck in a real shitter of a position. I didn't want to sleep on the couch because frankly, my back wasn't so hot and while the couch was fine for sitting and watching a movie on, it was going to be a chiropractor's dream to sleep on. But then again, taking her bed and forcing her to sleep on the couch didn't seem like the classiest thing to do and; coming on the heels of the first date rape movie, didn't seem like something that would improve my odds for date number three.

After much thought, I finally decided that my back would heal eventually, and voted for the couch.

"Here you go!" and with that, Julie tossed the pillows and blanket to me like we were turning a friggin' double play, and then promptly turned around and headed back into her bedroom.

I sat down on the couch in a state of disbelief, but tried to remind myself that this was only our second time together and I really couldn't expect her to sleep with me. I mean, after all, she was so out of my league to begin with, if she was ever going to sleep with me, she would be required by her union to make me wait at least until my balls were a lovely shade of purple. Then there was that kiss. Ahhh yes, that kiss. That was cool. I started focusing on the kiss again, as I untied my shoes and lay down on the couch. Slowly, the disappointment began to disappear and I was lost in thought. I threw the blanket over me and reached to turn the light off. As I did, I saw Julie coming toward me, wearing little red running shorts and a very tight tee-shirt.

"I still think the bed would have been more comfortable," she said as she crawled under the blanket and lay down next to me.

25

"You better do as you are told, you better listen to the radio."

—Elvis "Fathead" Costello

Things were going well. I had been moved out of the midnight to three shift at KCHO to the far more desirable ten in the morning jazz program. I was doing okay in my classes, especially since I was now a senior and didn't have to waste my time taking classes I didn't give a rat's ass about. And while Julie and I had not actually consummated our relationship that evening, I was pretty sure the roadmap had us pointed in the right direction.

Meanwhile, Jeff Pine, the large-testicle sounding guy who first showed me around the radio station, was doing the morning shift immediately preceding my show. One day I showed up a little earlier than normal and joined him on the air for the final hour of his gig. We hit it off immediately, and decided right then and there that we would approach the higher-ups about us teaming up to do the morning show.

"Kind of like all those great morning radio teams from the 60s and 70s—Hudson and Landry, Lohman and Barkley—those guys," I explained to Dr. Jenkins, the station's advisor.

Jenkins smiled, and reeled off a couple other radio names from the past. "Yeah, that was great radio," he mused. Then he stopped daydreaming and eyed Jeff and me with suspicion, his horribly permed hair sitting motionless on his head.

"I don't know, you guys," he said tapping his fingers on his desk. "We've never done anything like this before."

Jeff, who was always as mellow as mellow could be, gave Dr. Jenkins a confident smile. "I really think this is going to work, George. Just give us a chance."

"What does Steve think about it?" Dr. Jenkins asked, concerned that he might rule against the station manager's wishes.

"He's all for it," said Jeff, knowing that Steve would be all for any lame-ass idea as long as you provided him with enough dope.

Jenkins thought for a long time like this was an incredibly momentous decision—one that could change the entire face of the radio business as he knew it. Finally, he took a deep breath, closed his eyes, and slowly let the air exhale from his lungs.

"All right, here's what we'll do. We'll give you a chance. Keep it clean, make it funny, and we'll go from there," he concluded.

Well that was sure a ringing fucking endorsement. Nevertheless, Jeff and I walked out of Jenkins' office as happy as flies on dog shit.

"This is going to rock, Mitch," Jeff said. "We should probably get together and maybe discuss a few of your ideas for gags and skits and stuff, you know, before we go on."

I reviewed the extensive list of ideas that I had in my mind at that time for "gags and skits and stuff" and came up blank. "Sounds good!"

Our first show together was the following Monday. I had to be at the station by five-thirty in the morning and frankly, I've never been much of a morning person. Combined with the fact that it was now mid-November and colder than shit outside did not make me a very happy camper that first day.

Meanwhile, Jeff was overloading himself on coffee, so while he was wired for battle, I was yawning, grouchy and generally pissed off.

And it was only the first day.

We played it pretty straight for the first hour or so, mostly to give my brain a chance to wake up. We finally decided it was time to try our first little gag. Most big city morning radio shows have traffic reports and most have at least one guy flying around in a helicopter reporting about the latest tie-ups, accidents and general traffic crap. We thought it might be funny to do likewise, so we grabbed an old record that had the sound of a helicopter and did a phony traffic report.

"Let's go up to our eye in the sky Willie Bird for a look at traffic," said Jeff. "Willie, how are things looking this morning?"

With the "thwip, thwip, thwip" of the copter's rotors in the background I gave my report. "Well guys, things look pretty good on Broadway, but the traffic on Main Street seems to be really backing up right now. Several cars are caught up in this major blockage near Second Street. It's not a pretty sight."

"How long do you think the congestion is going to last?" asked a concerned Jeff.

"Tough to tell at this point," I replied. "There are just a lot of cars backed up and it's only getting worse. Could be a couple of hours before this clears up. Oh, wait a minute. The light changed. Everything's fine now."

And thus ended our first "gag, skit and stuff." We thought it sounded pretty funny so we got brave and tried some other ideas. But first, Jeff decided that was going to be the time that each of us were going to inherit new nicknames.

He clicked on the mike as a tune by jazz saxophonist David "Fathead" Newman wound down and said, "that was David "Fathead" Newman with "Concrete Jungle". Before that, Pat "Fathead" Methany with "Watercolors" and before Willie Bird's traffic report, we heard from Gato "Fathead" Barbieri and "Europa." From then on, every artist we played was "Fathead" and it seemed only natural at that point to change the name of the show from "Mitch and Jeff in the Morning" to "Fatheads in the Morning."

We met with Dr. Jenkins the next day and to say the least, his review of our initial effort was not brimming over with enthusiasm.

"Guys, I thought you were going to be doing some of the real funny stuff we talked about," he said. "It sounded more like a couple of guys goofing around for the most part."

Jeff kind of gave him a half smile. "Well George, it was our first show. I think you need to give us a little bit of a chance."

"And tell me, what was with all the "Fathead" stuff?" he asked. "I don't get it. Why were you calling everyone "Fathead"?

Jeff looked at me like I was going to have a well-researched, academically-supported answer to the question. Needless to say, I didn't.

"I thought it was funny," Jeff simply replied.

"Well, I don't understand it. Stop doing it. It doesn't make any sense."

It was at that point that Jeff and I began to realize maybe this wasn't such a hot idea after all.

"George, I really think you need to give us a chance to develop the show and not tell us right away what we can and can't do," Jeff bravely said. "Otherwise, we're going to be afraid to try anything."

Jenkins pondered what Jeff was saying.

"No," he said after much thought. "You guys promised to be funny and I just don't find the whole Fathead thing funny."

Jeff smiled, and then looked at me. "All right George, whatever you say."

The next day's installment of "Fatheads in the Morning" was more of the same—a few gags that fell flat, a few jokes that weren't all that funny, and a few skits that garnered few laughs. We managed to avoid meeting with Jenkins figuring that he would have nothing positive to say.

"We got to come up with something," said Jeff. "Don't you have any ideas?"

Three days into it, my mind was already DOA. Getting up at five in the morning was not my cup of tea, and whatever little creative juices I had, were not too motivated. Then, like the proverbial light bulb over the head, I had an idea.

I had heard a talk show featuring a guy giving advice on how to take care of various pets like dogs, cats, birds, etc. "What if we do a pet advice show where the guy giving the advice is the most obnoxious bastard in the world? We'll play some rinky-dink music in the background. It'll be hilarious!"

Jeff wasn't sure about the idea, but agreed to simply read what I put in front of him the next day. About an hour in, I told him it was time to do the skit.

Jeff put on some rinky-dink instrumental music in the background and let fly.

"It's time for Ask Dr. Fathead, Chico's only show offering expert advice on taking care of your pet," he said in a classic announcer voice. "Here's our first letter: Dear Dr. Fathead, my cat Muffie has a habit of turning in circles before she eats. Is this normal for a cat, or is my little Muffie performing for us? Signed, Muff lover."

"Dear Muff Lover," I said, in the most grating, annoying, obnoxious voice I could come up with. "Everyone knows that when a cat turns in circles before she eats, it's a sure sign it's about to DIE! Thanks for writing!"

And with that, Jeff and I cracked up.

"OK, here's our next letter," Jeff managed to say. "Dear Dr. Fathead, my parrot Harold's green feathers have turned a soft shade of red over the last couple of weeks. Is this something I should be worried about? Signed, Concerned."

I took a deep breath and tried not to look at Jeff. "Dear Concerned, everyone knows that when a parrot's green feathers turn a soft shade of red, it's a sure sign it's about to DIE! Thanks for writing!"

At this point, there was no way we were ever going to be able to continue. Both of us were laughing so hard inside we could barely breathe. Jeff finally clicked the mike back on and said "that's it for today's Ask Dr. Fathead. Tune in again tomorrow when Dr. Fathead will answer more of your pet questions!"

"Thanks for writing!" I added.

The minute the show was over, Jenkins was standing outside our door waiting for us.

"Shit," said Jeff. "I think we're in trouble."

The three of us walked silently down the hallway to his office, with Jeff and me playing the part of prisoners on their way to an execution. Jenkins sat down behind his desk, his powder blue vest looking as dorky as ever in combination with the worst fucking perm of all time. I was getting pissed just looking at him because I knew he was going to rip us a new one.

"Guys," he said seriously. "I need to talk to you about the Ask Dr. Fathead skit."

I looked at Jeff, waiting for him to offer up how the whole damn thing was my idea and that he was against it from the start.

"First of all," he lectured, "I thought I said to get rid of the whole Fathead thing." He looked seriously pissed.

Then suddenly he smiled broadly. "That," he said slowly, "was the funniest damn thing I've heard in a long time! It was hilarious! That's what you guys should be doing all the time! I can't wait to hear what you come up with tomorrow!"

Oh yeah, tomorrow. I think it was Irving Berlin who said the hardest thing about being successful is staying successful. Somewhere deep inside, I guess I was hoping that the Dr. Fathead skit would generate thousands of new ideas, but it didn't. Instead, Jenkins' words of praise simply made my asshole get tighter and tighter and my brain cells lock up. Between classes, work, and everything else, I was exhausted. Meanwhile, Jeff, who had been taking a whopping six units that semester, was contributing nothing but his large testicles, and mind you, they hadn't come up with a whole boatload of great ideas either.

Jeff and I walked upstairs and stood outside in the breezeway of the library. Jeff was giddy with excitement, so I knew what I was about to say was not going to be easy. I felt like I was a girl about to break up with this really nice guy.

"Jeff," I said, looking down at my feet. "I don't think I can keep this up. I'm exhausted, and I just don't have that many funny ideas."

Jeff was taken somewhat aback, especially since we had just received rave reviews from ol' permhead. "I don't understand. We rocked today. I know you've got other ideas."

And that in a nutshell was the problem. I didn't want to say to Jeff, "Look asshole, you're taking like no classes, you have no job, and yet you expect me to come up with all the ideas" so I just repeated the line about being too tired to keep this pace up.

After much discussion, I agreed to do another week of the show just so we could show Jenkins we could do it. We pulled off a couple of more decent skits—bogus interviews with Prince Charles and other poorly impersonated celebrities, but for the most part, Jenkins was right. We were just two guys goofing off for three hours.

26

"Julie, Julie, Julie, do you love me?"

—Bobby "Fathead" Sherman

I continued to see Julie when I could, and continued to not have sex with her. This, of course, was not by choice. She invited me over for dinner one night, and after watching another old movie, asked if I'd like to stay over. This time, I was much more decisive.

"Sure, but let's sleep in the bedroom this time," I said confidently.

"Sounds good to me," she said as she skipped off to the bathroom where I was positive she was slipping on a sexy piece of lingerie. Most likely, something in a soft purple with lace around the breasts and perhaps nothing but a small diamond shaped piece of material covering up her womanhood.

I took off my shirt but left my jeans on for the moment. I didn't want to seem too presumptuous. Plus, I didn't want to be standing there in my tighty-whiteys looking like a first class dork. And God knows, I didn't want to just crawl under the covers sans anything if that wasn't what she was thinking.

Finally, the bathroom door opened and Julie emerged wearing black running shorts and a pretty tight powder blue shirt. Her breasts looked beautiful, but my eagle eyes also noticed that they were still held captive by the almighty bra. Now I was in a real pickle. This outfit did not exactly say, "ravage my body you tremendously handsome man." It was more like, "not now, not tomorrow, and perhaps, not ever."

Julie made her way to the other side of the room, closed the curtains, and turned off all the lights except for the small lamp next to her bed. She pulled back the covers and climbed in.

"Boy, I'm pooped," she said.

Great. Just another in the long line of boner killers. It goes well with:
a) "Is it in?"
b) "You remind me of my father."

c) "Oh God, please forgive me for what I'm about to do ..."

I had no idea what to do. Her outfit was by no means an open invitation. If I took my pants off and climbed in with just my underwear on, that might cause a reaction ranging anywhere from amusement to anger. Or worse, another boner killer like, "just what do you think you're doing?" I didn't want to do anything that might possibly offend her, so I just climbed into bed wearing my blue jeans.

Julie leaned over and gave me a quick kiss.

"Goodnight," she said.

I looked at that beautiful smile, and for the moment, forgot how Goddamn uncomfortable I was lying in bed wearing blue jeans.

That whole night was a disaster as I tossed and turned, desperately trying to get comfortable. If I had just an ounce of intelligence, I would have simply taken my jeans off and if Julie questioned it at all, simply explained that I was unable to sleep with 501s riding up my ass. But I didn't. So instead I spent a miserable night sweating underneath the covers and staring at the ceiling.

The next morning Julie woke up and went to the bathroom. When she came out, she still had on the black running shorts and the very tight blue shirt. But now I noticed something different. The bra had been removed and had been replaced by a lovely pair of nipples poking through the shirt.

She climbed back into bed and despite our morning breath, we started to kiss. I lifted up her shirt to reveal what could almost be referred to as the perfect set of ta-tas. Meanwhile, my jeans were getting all twisted around me under the covers, so I thought if ever there was a time to take them off, this was it. I lay down on my back and started to unbutton my jeans, but before I could, Julie was on top of me. We started kissing again and my hands reached down and cupped her ass through the black nylon of her shorts. This was going great! This was going to be awesome! If I could only get my fucking jeans off before I came.

My hands went up her back and down to her perfect ass again. I couldn't have asked for a better situation except that I was trapped under the covers and my jeans were cutting off most of the circulation to my lower extremities. I needed to somehow, very smoothly, get Julie off of me for a couple of seconds so I could get my flippin' pants off and get out from under the covers without ruining the mood. Of course, I could have simply said, "Excuse me Julie, but would you mind removing your exquisite ass from on top of me and placing it within easy reach for just a moment whilst I slip these chinos off?"

But I didn't need to.

Suddenly, Julie stopped kissing me. She looked me deep in the eyes and said, "We have plenty of time for this, okay?"

What was I supposed to say? "Uh no, we don't have plenty of time for this. We need to get this done right now. So get off me, take those friggin' shorts off, and let's rock!"

"Uh ... okay."

She smiled. "You want some breakfast?" she asked, as she climbed off me and off the bed.

"Sure, that would be great," I said, resigned to my fate.

I had never had a woman make me breakfast before, unless of course you count my mom, and that flat out doesn't count. Julie whipped me up some bacon and eggs, a couple slices of toast and a glass of orange juice like an old pro. She brought it all out to me on a platter, put it on the small coffee table and turned on a football game on TV. I almost made the mistake of leaving her a tip when I was done it was so damn good.

"So what are you doing today?" I innocently asked, after bringing my plate into the kitchen.

"Not much," she said. "Gotta go grocery shopping and that sort of thing, and then me and some friends are going out tonight. How about you?"

"Believe it or not, I'm actually going to study for a test I have Monday," I laughed, almost not believing my own words. "It's a rare occurrence, but one that I feel should be done occasionally just to sooth my conscience."

I headed home a little while later wearing a smile as wide as Big Chico Creek. This was going to be a marathon, I thought, kind of like with Daron, but with a finish line that was at least within sight. I knew, deep down, that we hadn't reached that point of exclusivity yet, and the subject had never been brought up, but I was pretty confident that I was the only guy on Julie's radar screen at the moment.

I was also pretty confident that the Cubs were a lock to win the World Series that year.

And so it came to pass that the ugly head of reality came up and bit me on the ass. All right, my metaphors are a little screwed up, but the idea is that things didn't work out the way I planned. That night, my friend Matt decided to actually venture out for a night on the town and apparently ran into Julie, a fact he couldn't wait to tell me about the next morning when he called.

"So I saw Julie last night," he calmly said.

"Really?" I replied, acting none too concerned. "Where at?"

"Down at Cabo's Nightclub. She was at the Greg Kihn concert."

Seemed harmless enough, I thought. But Matt couldn't let it go at that.

"She looked very nice," he continued.

"She always does," I confidently replied, not wanting to play whatever little game he had going on.

"Yep, real nice. Was wearing this kind of tight black dress."

"Anything else you want to tell me?" I asked.

"Oh yeah, she was with this guy that looked like Robert Redford ..."

I froze.

"... only better looking!" And with that, Matt began convulsing in gales of laughter, truly enjoying whatever internal agony I was going through.

I had always been a fan of the old "Twilight Zone" series, especially the intro where Rod Serling said, "there's a signpost up ahead, your next stop, the Twilight Zone!" Well, this was my signpost, and it certainly wasn't reading "Welcome to Paradise." This head-on crash into reality only became clearer when I made the mistake of stopping by Julie's house unannounced a couple weeks before winter break. In the back of my mind, I still felt that I was in the running, though once I found out more about our Robert Redford clone—a pretty boy named Chuck who I had casually known through my job at the info booth—I realized that my chances were only marginal. But I had invested too much time and energy and wet dreams into this relationship to give up so easy.

I had been out with Steve the K, Hammer and a few other guys, and we were coincidentally walking down Second Avenue near her house on a crisp December evening. I told the guys that I was going to stop by Julie's, and I would catch up with them later. I stopped outside her house, looking around to see if there were any unfamiliar cars parked nearby. The lights were on in the front window, so it was obvious that someone was home. I quietly made my way up the walkway to her front porch. I ever so gently tip-toed on to the wooden porch and tried to peer in the window, but my view was blocked by the curtains. Ah, what the hell, I thought, as I knocked on the door.

"Come on in!" I heard Julie yell from behind the door.

I opened the door, and there was Julie and her two roommates all sitting around decorating the Christmas tree.

"Hey!" I said.

"Hi, Mitch," said Julie, acting as if she'd seen a ghost.

And right then, Chuck strolled in from the kitchen with a string of popcorn ready to hang on the tree. My heart sunk into my stomach, and I felt like the biggest chicken in the world had just laid the biggest egg in the world on my face.

"Uh, Mitch, you know Chuck, right?" Julie said as casually as she could, considering she might as well have been introducing Lincoln to John Wilkes Booth.

"Yeah ... hey, Chuck," I said unenthusiastically.

Meanwhile, Mr. Pretty Boy was too busy being wonderful looking to realize that this was supposed to be an uncomfortable situation. He looked up at me, jutted his perfectly square jaw out, flashed a smile using all sixty-four of his teeth, and greeted me like he was running for political office.

"Hey, Mitch, nice to see you again," he said as he sat down next to Julie. The message was clear. This was their Christmas party and I was the Grinch.

"All right … well … I was just walking by so I thought I'd pop in," I babbled, trying to extricate myself from the situation. "I'll see you all later, I guess." I looked at Julie and while her eyes were slightly apologetic, the rest of her seemed comfortable in the situation. It was kind of like she was saying, "you're a nice guy, Mitch, but let's face it; Chuck looks like Robert Redford."

Only better looking.

27

"Women need a reason to have sex. Men just need a place."

—*Billy "Fathead" Crystal*

Her name was Carol Russo.

I had met Carol while working in the information booth in the BMU. She was a fairly attractive gal with nearly white hair, light blue eyes and soft white skin. And she liked to have sex. It was like I was dating an albino rabbit. Our relationship was based purely on sex because except for the few times that we talked at the information booth, I really never saw her in broad daylight. She invited me over one day, and one thing led to another and there we were bouncing up and down on her waterbed like boats in a hurricane. The next night she called me at the apartment and asked me to come over. I did, and after a few pleasantries, and the odd ritual of saying hello to her pet pig, we'd be at it.

Now since I wasn't exactly oversexed at that point, this was all a whale of fun. I wasn't a big fan of staying over for the night, not because I'm one of those guys that likes to be alone afterwards, but because I've never been able to sleep on a waterbed. Whoever the genius was that came up with the concept of a waterbed must never have had a back problem.

I tried staying over the first few times, but in the morning it literally felt like a knife was sticking right into my solar plexus.

"Can't move … can't breathe," I gasped one morning.

"Can you fuck?" asked Carol.

But even the best things in life can get tiresome if done too often. After awhile, I started going over when she called, not because I was interested in having sex, but because I wanted to listen to a Jackson Browne album she had and I didn't have the money to buy it.

Finally, I started coming up with reasons why I couldn't go over.

"Hi, Mitch," she said one night on the phone, "can you come over?"

"Uhhh, I got a lot of homework and stuff, I don't think so."

Carol laughed. "You're so funny. I know you never do homework. Come on, come over. I got a surprise for you!"

The big surprise turned out to be a line of cocaine as long as my arm. I hadn't realized Carol was a cokehead prior to this, but now everything suddenly made perfect sense. She took a big hit and asked me if I wanted some. As usual, I declined the generous offer.

"Great, more for me," she said before pushing me onto the bed.

◆   ◆   ◆

I hadn't seen Janet for months, but I had heard she was going to be at a party at one of our friend's house. It was a good old time with most of the regular crew there including Hammer, Steve the K., Matt, Beth, Vickie, Cathy and Janet's brother Tim. Also there was Teresa Hightman, one of the girls that lived with Beth. Teresa was a genuine, one hundred percent, honest-to-goodness, whack-job. She had pale skin, freckles, red hair, and little old lady hands that shook constantly. She was an emotional wreck as well, laughing her ass off one second, crying it off the next. She had been in the dorms with us at Shasta, and had been "in love" with each and every one of us at some point during the year. Not a one of us took her up on her offer of love, but we all knew the opportunity was there. Of course, we also knew that if we did sleep with her, we would have to blow our brains out the next day to avoid the repercussions.

So I'm at this party and for the first time in a long while, I'm having a few drinks. OK, not a few … a lot. The music was blaring and here comes Teresa, all shaking and pale and God knows what else.

"Hey Mitch, you want to dance?" she asked innocently enough.

I looked around hoping, praying, that someone was in desperate need of CPR and that would be a bona-fide excuse for not being able to rock-around-the-clock with Teresa.

"Uhhh," I mumbled, "not right now Teresa, I gotta go talk to Tim," as if Tim and I had anything to share but my longing for his sister and his hatred of me.

"OK, I guess," she said with a look of confusion.

Two seconds later, Janet came up from behind me and tapped me on the shoulder.

"Hey stranger, haven't seen you in a long time," she said. We gave each other a quick hug and then she dropped the bomb.

"Want to dance?"

"You bet!" I said without hesitation. Now like most guys, I'm a lousy dancer, so normally I wouldn't have just jumped out on to the dance floor—it's far too embarrassing. I usually tried to avoid it at all costs for fear of being ridiculed. But I was drunk, so I didn't give a shit what other people thought of me.

The next thing I knew, I felt a wave of cold rocky mountain spring water being dumped on my head. I turned around and there was Teresa, her hand shaking, holding an empty beer cup.

"Fuck you!" she shouted. "You wouldn't dance with me, but Janet walks into the room and you don't waste a second before you're dancing with her!"

"Jesus, Teresa, why'd you pour a beer on me?" I asked all innocently.

"Because you're a bastard!" And with that clear and well-thought out explanation, she grabbed Hammer's cup and threw that on me as well.

"Damn it, Teresa, why'd you take my beer?" asked Hammer.

While Teresa was circling the cuckoo's nest, Janet and I were cracking up. Teresa went flying out the door, yelling a string of obscenities that would have made Long John Silver blush. By now, the beer was running down my back making nice with my Fruit of the Looms. Janet suggested I go clean up before we continued our dance of amour, so I headed off to the bathroom which I thought was somewhere near the kitchen.

Tim stopped me as I was stumbling around, looking for the can.

"Mitch," he said, putting his hand on my chest. "That wasn't very nice the way you treated Teresa."

"What are you, drunk?" I asked.

"Of course I am," he said. "But I saw what happened. When are you going to realize that you and Jan are not happening?"

"We were just dancing, Tim, it was no big deal. And Jesus, Teresa's a fuckin' nut case!"

"I just don't think you should treat people like that," he said all serious like, poking me in the chest. I couldn't tell if it was really him, or the twelve beers he had most likely consumed speaking at this point.

"Tim, relax—and how about you mind your own business, okay?" I said. This was definitely the beers talking on my end.

With that Tim stopped poking me in the chest and instead gave me a healthy shove. My feet went out from under me, which considering my state of inebriation, could have been accomplished by a light breeze. I banged my forehead on the cheap-ass coffee table that was there, and the next thing I knew, I had a nice little gash in my head.

"Jesus, Tim, what the fuck?" was the best I could come up with.

Tim helped me up, apologized for his transgression, and then went into the kitchen like nothing happened.

"Hey, Mitch," Hammer yelled, "someone's on the phone for you."

I had no idea who would have known I was at this party, but I managed to make my way into the kitchen to answer the phone.

"Hello?" I said.

"Hey, Mitch, it's Carol! I thought you were coming over tonight."

"Oh, yeah," I said, completely forgetting that I had mentioned to her something about stopping by at some point. "Guess I forgot."

"Well, why don't you come over right now? I've got some wine and I'm wearing a robe and nothing else!"

I wiped the blood off my face with the dishtowel. "I don't think that would be such a great idea right now," I offered.

"Why not? I want to see you!"

"Well to be honest; I'm covered in beer, I'm bleeding, I'm drunk, I smell, and I don't want to ride my bike across town," I said, not even including the little fact that Janet was at this party.

"But I want to see you!" she pleaded. I wasn't sure who was more pathetic at this point—Carol for wanting to sleep with a guy that looked like he just climbed out of the sewer, or me for not being able to say no to meaningless sex.

"See you in a couple of minutes," I finally said despondently.

I guess it was me.

28

"The future is much like the present, only longer."

—Dan "Fathead" Quisenberry

By the time the end of May rolled around, I was ready to leave school. I still loved the town and the general concept of going to college, but I was tired of the routine of going to class and taking tests. I was ready to try my hand in the world of professional radio or whatever the future held for me. My family made their one and only visit to Chico for the graduation ceremonies, fortunately bypassing a stopover at my place of residence. Though Steve, Greg and I had slightly upgraded our living accommodations over the Palace on Sixth Avenue, it would have still been enough give my mom an aneurism.

At the time, each school would hold their own graduation, a truly brilliant concept in that it spared everyone from having to sit through the litany of names of all the graduating seniors being read starting with Anthony A. Aardvark.

The Communications Department somehow managed to get the best spot of all for its ceremony, Laxson Auditorium. Julie and I, and a few other friends from the radio station, all decided to sit together so that we could enjoy this magical, momentous occasion as a group. We filed into Laxson wearing our black graduation garb topped off with those goofy mortarboard hats they make you wear. I always wondered who the genius was that came up with that hat for such a supposedly important and dignified occasion as graduation. It was like the dude was a dropout who got his revenge on all the "smart" kids by designing a hat that would make them look as dignified as a Hell's Angel at a church social.

Anyway, we all filed in with the students sitting up front and the parents relegated to the back and the upper balcony. The first speech began, with the speaker blathering on about the "future" and how we had the capacity to "change the world." Somehow I doubted that my ability to spin records or ad-lib into a microphone would accomplish all that, but what the hell, it was a nice thought. After a couple more yawners, they finally started calling our names. When we had originally picked up our graduation gown and other accoutrements, they had included an index card in which we were to legibly write our full name. We were then to hand the index card to the speaker who would then announce our name. To me, this was just asking for trouble as I could imagine some of the creative "names" some folks could come up with, but bless their maturing hearts, there wasn't a "Harry P. Ness" or similar name called out.

It was finally our rows' turn to get in line and receive our phony-baloney diplomas one right after another. They didn't give you the real diploma at that point because grades weren't final, and they don't want to hand out the old sheepskin to some doof who just nailed straight F's in his final term. I watched Julie gracefully make her way across the stage, admiring her beauty and poise, knowing that she would be successful in whatever walk of life she chose. Then it was my turn. I handed the speaker the little white card with my name on it. He spoke in a clear, booming voice, "Mitchell Shawn Cox" as I nervously walked across the stage. There were a few hoots and hollers from friends in the audience, and of course, mom had moved up to the front, camera in hand, snapping photo after photo. And then it was over. I was unofficially a college graduate.

Julie and I returned to our seats and cheered on the others we knew as they made the short walk into their future, all of them happy yet petrified that this chapter in their life was now over. You could see it in their eyes. They had grown up over the past few years, but at this precise moment in time, they were squinting through the glare of lights, trying desperately to catch a sight of their parents and that feeling of security.

After the final graduate made their way across the stage, Julie and I stood up and headed for the exit and the bright Chico sunshine that awaited all of us. I knew Chuck would be out there waiting for her, so I asked for a kiss before I had to see her and numb-nuts get all lovey-dovey. I wanted to hold the line behind us up with a long, passionate, toe-curling smooch, but instead got a quick peck on the lips, a hug, and a "thanks, I'll never forget you," which in the long run, was probably more meaningful. I eventually found my parents and my brother in the crowd of humanity and after the customary round of photos were taken, it was time to head out.

"We're very proud of you, Mitch," mom said, giving me a hug that only a mom can give. Dad gave me a hug as well and patted me on the back until my spine needed to be readjusted. Then Kerry reached out to shake my hand.

"Way to go, Poo," he said.

God I hated it when he called me that.

978-0-595-46565-1
0-595-46565-X

Printed in the United States
130454LV00012B/145-165/A

9 780595 465651

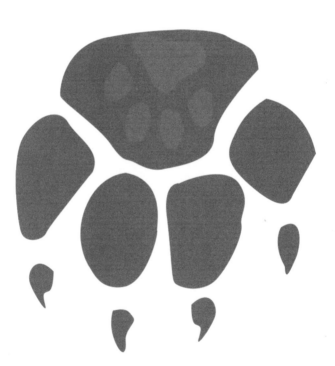

ABOUT THE COVER: When my boys were young, one of their favorite movies was Disney's animated classic "The Lion King." In one scene, Simba, the young and precocious son of King Mufasa, steps into a paw imprint left by his much bigger and wiser father. The contrast is not lost on the young cat. Simba's paw seemed so small and insignificant compared to his father's. It was a powerful reminder to Simba that he had a lot of growing ahead before he would reach his potential and assume the mantle of king.

I think each one of us is like Simba. There is the person we currently are – and there is the person God has created us to become. When it comes to our God-given calling and spiritual giftedness, we must embrace the journey of growth that comes with reaching our potential. We must grow in our character, our competency, and our clarity.

Jesus was called the Lion of Judah (Revelation 5:5). We are called to be made new in his image (Romans 8:29). God is glorified when we follow Jesus and allow him to mold and grow us into little "lions of Judah." Your paw print may be small at the moment – but don't despair, growth will come as you walk with Jesus. Lion cubs are cute, but Lion Kings shape the world. Which will you choose?

Dedicated
To Everyone Who Ever Took a
Chance on God
for the Sake of Others